# The National Times

Fabian M.C. Kuykendall

Published by Fabian M.C. Kuykendall, 2024.

THE NATIONAL TIMES

**First edition. February 20, 2024.**



ISBN: 979-8224685387

Written by Fabian M.C. Kuykendall.

# Table of Contents

# PREFACE

Like most people in America, I'm very opinionated. Unlike most people, I don't impose my two cents on every platform of social media. My written opinion is, instead, reserved for projects such as this. In these pages, I speak candidly about racism, political division, sexuality, artificial intelligence, and—among other things—mental illness. My intent with this project was to give my opinion based on facts instead of concocting facts based on my opinion.

By no means am I a certified professional, nor do I consider myself to be an expert on any topic. However, I do have strong opinions on such topics, which I feel the need to share. Some people will perceive my views as being, at times, contradictory. I attribute this to the fact that I'm always able to see both sides of an argument while attempting to avoid neutrality.

This project was largely conceived during the eras of Black Lives Matter, Make America Great Again, and the Covid pandemic. As you'll notice, the topic of race comes up often. This isn't about playing the "race card," it's about telling the truth, and the truth is that race has become a major part of everything that we do, see, hear, read, think, and say. In fact, my chapters on society, politics, religion, entertainment, and law are all correlated by race.

As a Black person, I write from a Black perspective. I can't be expected to speak for all people, I can only give an account of my experience. This Black perspective should not be viewed as a bias against those who can't relate to it. It's important to me that people of different persuasions be able to see life through the eyes of each other to gain a full understanding of the American experience.

This project was, at times, emotionally exhausting to write. I had to take many extended breaks in production for the sake of my mental health. I found motivation to complete this project through what I feel is the importance of speaking my piece. There's so much to unpack regarding the American nation, and while a lot of it is hard to digest, it needs to be addressed.

To be clear, I'm not "woke," I'm enlightened. I'm educated and opinionated. I don't have any political motivation whatsoever. My objective is to shed light on the uncomfortable truths of the American experience that often get politicized. My hope is that you, the reader, will gain something from these *opinion* pieces and be able to understand, acknowledge, and respect my opinion.

# CHAPTER 1 - SOCIETY & CULTURE

---

## *The Ethos of Now: American Culture in the Information Age*

Today's culture begins and ends with social media. It is our obsession and guidebook through life. We live and see life through smartphones, tablets, and laptops to fulfill a self-conceived social media obligation. At any given moment, you can expect to find someone soliciting a specific response—or any attention at all—from their posts on Twitter (X), Facebook, Instagram, TikTok, etc. Even a few seconds of silence is unbearable for the vast majority of people who compulsively pull out their phones at the slightest risk of awkward aloneness. It seems that we have to fill every solitary moment with digital entertainment because we're not comfortable with ourselves.

Mystery is terribly underrated, and normal isn't normal anymore. Normal is people sheepishly following trends in order to fit in—people follow followers. We live in a beige society where we are required to conform in order to be successful and to be accepted. Depending on the kind of life that you lead, one might wonder: Is it worth it to be yourself? Society says that you're not normal if you don't follow the majority. If you're not completely consumed by social media and don't have a page on every major social network, then you're an outcast. Really?

Privacy is no longer valued in today's society. Public restroom urinals no longer have dividers, many companies base hires on social media profiles, and—thanks to smartphones—people can record you whenever they want to without your consent. There's a ridiculous expectation to share every pointless, minute detail of our lives. From the moment they enter the world, children now have social media profiles. The more irresponsible parents even turn their preschool children into performers whose pictures and videos are used to entertain millions of strangers.

It seems that most of society is eager to turn even the most serious moments of their lives into entertainment for everyone else. Reality television is a prime example of the shameless thirst for fame and attention that overshadows any logic or dignity. There are instances on social media of posts made immediately subsequent to supposed suicide attempts. Why is there such an onus to overshare? Also, why is it that people would rather film positive live events with their phones instead of just experiencing them? It seems that the more we connect digitally, the more disconnected we become.

We encourage individuality, but there's still an unspoken expectation that everyone should come from the same template. Men should be into sports and drinking, women should be into fashion and shopping, and everyone should be married with children by a certain age. When someone doesn't fit into this mainstream stereotype, they're seen as some sort of weird pariah. In today's society, there is no individuality. Just look at social media, everyone looks and acts exactly the same. One image fits all.

Social vanity has intensified to extreme levels of cosmetic alterations. Far too many of today's women treat their bodies like their wardrobes, making alterations based on what's in fashion. They inflate their asses to cartoonish proportions with injections and Brazilian butt lifts, and reduce their faces to a gaunt visage with buccal fat removal surgery. A robotic, paralyzed, plastic expression is inexplicably the most sought after look. Everyone has to be airbrushed, filtered, and Photoshopped in pictures and in real life. Celebrities and the media continue to send the message that we're not supposed to look human anymore.

Online dating was once taboo—mostly seen as a desperate embarrassment. We now live in a "swipe right" society where people can basically order dates like clothing or fast food. We've gotten to the point where we'd rather meet people online than in person. Social convention has deteriorated to outright irreverence. It's disturbing how comfortable people have become with "ghosting." It's rude and it's cowardly, but—since it's trendy—that doesn't seem to matter. Ghosting is like the new cheating, although cheating takes commitment. I don't understand why people would rather put their time and effort into cheating on someone instead of just ending the relationship and being free.

I think that open marriages/relationships will become commonplace in the not-so-distant future. Monogamy seems almost unnatural at this point as an ever-declining number of people remain faithful to their spouses. More and more women choose to allow their men to cheat just to keep him happy and to keep him in their lives. These open marriages and relationships always seem to be for the benefit of the man. Today, marriage is more of a business deal—a social formality.

Many of us are raising our children to be physically, mentally, academically, socially, financially, and literally superior to their peers. There's an army of tiger moms and dads who impose strict discipline and damaging perfectionism on their kids. This method of parenting is always for the parents' benefit—to make them look good. They hover above these kids at all times, giving them little room to breathe—let alone make a mistake. They also hold them to unattainable standards that the parents themselves can't even reach. Meanwhile, the children they raise are likely to rebel as young adults and become a problem for society.

Generation Z—also known as Zoomers—generally seems to be lacking in motivation and ambition. In the workforce, many of them simply don't want to work. They have a spoiled, entitled mentality that makes them believe that they shouldn't have to work. They even started the asinine trend of "quiet quitting," which is basically ghosting their employer. It's weak and irresponsible, and they don't even give thought to the future repercussions. However, it's not just Zoomers; almost no one wants to work anymore. People would rather beg on the streets than to get an actual job. Actually, many people see shameless solicitation as an actual job for which they even have a schedule. They often don't even bother to look the part of an actual vagrant, yet we keep feeding the ducks.

Many Millennials and Zoomers are obsessed with the word *Illuminati*. They love to attach its *symbolism* to people and events in order to create their own paranoid conspiracy theories. They attempt to condemn any person—especially a (Black) celebrity—who is very successful, talented, and highly regarded by insisting that the person must have sold their soul or is a devil-worshiper. What's really annoying is the self-righteous attitudes of those who condemn this alleged devil-worship when they couldn't care less about God or religion. They're often laughably misinformed about what the Illuminati actually is—basing most of their opinion off of what they learned from a YouTube video.

Advancements in technology have cursed us with option overload. From the streaming services of television, movies, and music to technology itself, there's simply too much from which to choose. We've become so spoiled with modern perks that it's overwhelming. We've developed a dependency in which we've lost our connection to the analog world. There's a frustrating irony when technology that was supposed to simplify our lives only makes them more complicated. It makes some of us appreciate—and long for—the simpler days when there was less reliance on technology.

The zeitgeist has us hypnotized by a mind-numbing 24-hour news cycle. It's sickening how the news and other media want to inundate us with negativity. There's never a break from bad news, and it's always sensationalized for the sake of drama and provocation. On top of politics, war, and crime, we also constantly have to hear about the latest objects of cancel culture. So many wealthy celebrities and executives get "cancelled" because they can't resist making clever racist, sexist, or just plain ignorant remarks on social media. For as many times as it's happened, I don't understand why these people don't know any better. Also, the world seems to be overrun with Karens, entitled, insufferable shrews—usually White women—who, apparently, live to cause trouble for people who mind their own business. There isn't a peaceful place left in this world.

Why is it that most Americans seem to place a higher value on the life of an animal or pet than that of a human? We completely anthropomorphize our pets and treat them as our children or "fur babies." It seems that people are consumed with the unwavering loyalty and devotion they receive from a pet—especially a dog. Most people are jaded by society when they become adults, so they develop a codependent relationship with an animal that can't hurt them emotionally. Pets are important, but—by law—they're property. Therefore, I'm confounded when we give so much effort and money to rescue dogs and cats while ignoring the ongoing crisis of children who are starving and suffering.

Pets are so beloved and pampered that sometimes—between pet and human—it's hard to tell who the owner is. People who don't share this obsessive adoration for pets are somehow seen as almost un-American. Many pet owners take offense to those who don't worship their pets. To not shower them with attention and affection is to commit a hate crime. What too many pet owners don't realize is that it's not always the case that people don't like dogs and cats. Many people are allergic or sometimes they simply don't want to be around them. Why is that a problem?

Most people seem to be too self-involved to be empathetic and compassionate toward humanity. It's so easy for us to go about our busy, trivial schedules while ignoring—or never even noticing—those in need; that's part of the reason why homelessness is such an epidemic in America. Unfortunately, because humanitarianism isn't as common as it should be, the motives behind it sometimes come into question. An act of goodwill and philanthropy should not be seen as a political statement, it should be a societal norm. We shouldn't be so out of touch with humanity that such a thing has to carry an agenda.

The benevolence of charity is far too often tarnished by self-indulgent egotism. The upper-class elite frequently gather to pat themselves on the back with opulent bashes under the guise of philanthropic fund-raising. Their hedonistic grandstanding overshadows the important causes they claim to hold so dearly. On top of that, there are so-called charities that build personal wealth by exploiting those in need. They seem to carry out this immoral behavior with a "*some* help is better than none" mentality.

The social obligations presented to us by most holidays are ridiculous and overvalued. These holidays force us to buy certain gifts—or do certain things—and basically dictate how we live our lives, all at the risk of being socially excluded. Another obligatory custom is saying "bless you" or "God bless you" when someone sneezes. This has turned into such a mandate that some people get offended if you don't say it. Customary or not, it makes no sense at all. Saying "bless you" isn't going to save a person from the imminent death they'll apparently suffer when they sneeze.

Americans seem to thrive on pity. Reality competition shows exploit this idea ad nauseam. We're so quick to tell our sob stories to make people feel obligated to like us. Meanwhile, we're constantly on the lookout for other people's flaws and fuckups so that we can feel better about ourselves. We all have sob stories because we all go through hard times. No one's story is so unique that they deserve special treatment. It's a shameful embarrassment to seek pity for personal gain, and it's an embarrassing shame to take pleasure in the detriment of others.

It's been said that many countries see the general friendly, happy disposition of Americans as "forced" or "fake." I've noticed that it's almost customary for us to laugh at each other's jokes. Whether someone is funny or not, it's seen as rude for us not to offer at least a pity laugh and disregard how we really feel. It's also common for us to exaggerate everything from story details, cadence, facial expressions, and reactions, all for the amusement of others. We always feel the need to entertain and be entertained. There doesn't seem to be a setting in which we're allowed to be our true selves.

Americans love to complain, even though—when we look at the big picture—we have so little to complain about. As Americans, we often fail to recognize our American privilege and how blessed we are to live in such a thriving country filled with opportunity. When we turn our attention away from the negative and the trivial, we're able to see the beauty of living in America. We have so much information at our disposal with which to enrich our country and fortify ourselves as Americans. Ultimately, it's up to us to decide how we want to define our culture.

## *Rabbit Hole: The Soulless Vacuum of Social Media*

The world is a network of social connects. It's a cyber-social nexus which—in the digital age—is how we relate. Social media is a gathering place for exhibitionists and voyeurs. It's a breeding ground for scammers and catfishers. It's a cluster of platforms to which we dedicate hours upon hours of wasted time, and—for millions of us—it's an all-consuming addiction. This addiction is caused by an endless search for validation that ultimately leaves us with a void.

The global obsession with social media reached critical mass with Facebook. It began as a way to connect the world in a positive way. Gradually, we began to saturate our book of faces to give the illusion of social wealth. When Facebook gave birth to Instagram, we had a concentrated outlet for engaging in self-obsessed behavior. Now—every minute of every day—we're able to see each other's lives through pictures. People are usually less than they seem, that's why they post pictures to show a life better than yours. They crave your attention for their self-esteem. There's no telling what goes on behind their closed doors.

Twitter (X)—the collective comments section of the Internet—is basically a deposit box for everyone's two cents. It's also a soapbox for self-righteous rants and tangents. More than that, it's become the platform of choice for trolls to spew their hateful invectives. The anonymity gives these social media Mafiosos an exaggerated sense of bravery. Twitter (X) has become a sounding board for hate speech and political agendas that challenges the idea of freedom of speech. More than any other platform, it seems to divide the masses. Someone always manages to tweet something that inevitably comes back to bite them. It's baffling how so many people still don't understand that once we post something, it exists in perpetuity.

TikTok seems to be the tastemaker that decides what we should all be obsessed with. It has people constantly trying to outdo each other to come up with the next microtrend. Its influence on pop culture is substantial and a bit scary. Social media is flooded with self-proclaimed content creators, creatives, and influencers—many of whom have become millionaires through the medium.

It's a shame that they make more money than doctors, teachers, first responders, even the president of the United States. So many kids don't aspire to noble professions now because they no longer have to. They know very well that they can get rich and famous by posting frivolous content on social media.

We're lost in a culture that insists that a certain number of followers or likes constitutes a major accomplishment. This culture follows the mandate of constant self-promotion. It even goes beyond self-promotion to the point of self-worship, which has grown into a disturbing obsession for the masses. Some people even stoop to the pathetic low of buying likes and followers on social media. It's basically a culture of competing for attention with desperate attempts to go viral. Social media trends have turned into trivial obligation. Every day, we're expected to perpetuate the digital chain mail of social media challenges. One of the more asinine challenges—the Tide pod challenge—involved swallowing a small ball of laundry detergent to basically see if you'd survive.

So many people post and repost memes on social media about how they don't have time for nonsense or about how they generally "don't care," but they contradict themselves by dedicating so much of their time and effort to share these posts. Somehow, they care enough to keep saying they don't care. Everyone seems to think that it's such a good look to give this illusion of being immortally unbothered. I really don't understand the fake disinterest from hypocrites who always have an opinion. They clearly worry about what everyone else thinks of them. They don't seem to understand that we know they're human, and it's human to care—if only the world cared a little less about social media.

At its best, social media can be a unifier that helps people connect with old friends and lost family members—I found my baby brother through MySpace, and was able to meet him for the first time in about twenty years. At its worst, social media is a troll's paradise. It's the perfect playground for misery to find its company. Miserable people prey on others through online bullying and harassment, financial scams, and catfish dating. Social media is dangerous because no one is exactly as they seem. Everyone hides behind avatars and aliases, so you never know who they really are. How can you truly connect when you can't trust your connection?

Personally, I believe that social media brings out the worst in humanity and needs to be cancelled. It encourages narcissism, magnifies insecurities, and exacerbates mental illness. Granted, it does have some benefits, but it generally does more harm than good. More and more people are being driven to take a break from social media because of all of its negativity. It's bad for self-esteem, saturated with fakeness, and even pushes people to the point of suicide, yet there are algorithms designed to keep you addicted to its dark, insidious stronghold.

We're hypnotized under the mind control of social media. Ruled by a magnetic force, we're permanently affixed to our phones. Fighting through neck pain and eye strain, we freely give in to the compulsive need to be connected. Many of us experience physical withdrawal symptoms when we try to give up this addiction. We're in dire need of a social media detox. Whatever it is that we're looking for, we'll never find it online. Even with billions of likes, shares, and re-tweets, the void will still remain.

## *The Asterism: America's Obsession with Celebrity & Royalty*

Why are we so desperate to be a part of the celebrity asterism? Everyone seems to have an unquenchable thirst for attention and adulation. In this era of social media psychosis, people don't just want engagements or popularity, they want to be worshiped. Everyone calls themselves an "influencer" to make themselves look more important than they really are. To these so-called influencers and their followers, everything is "iconic," and everyone is a "legend" or a "GOAT." These terms are so overused and misused that they've lost all meaning. Greatness is being redefined as the lowest common denominator.

Our main goal in life isn't just to be successful or wealthy, it's to be envied. It's all about pomp and circumstance, that's why we spend so much time playing "look at me" on social media. This pretentious obligation has millions of easily influenced people using designer labels to justify their worth—It's funny how people say that they don't like to be labeled, yet they wear designer labels like badges of honor. To them, such a trifling level of pageantry is mandatory because expensive things aren't worth having unless everyone else sees them. So many of us would rather live beyond our means and go bankrupt just for the sake of presenting the illusion of celebrity.

In society, we obsessively aspire to VIP treatment and first-class accommodations. There seems to be a desperate need for us to feel like we're more important than other people. I don't understand why any respectable restaurant, airline, or other establishment wouldn't provide the same high level of service to everyone. Instead, they prefer to entitle some people and segregate others by assigning them a level of importance. As humans, who are we to decide which humans are more important than others? Why are we so insistent on branding everything with classism?

It's amazing how accustomed and expectant we are to being pampered. When we dine at restaurants, it's almost customary for us to treat their staff like our own personal servants. What compels us to diminish service workers by referring to them as "the help?" The fact that we think this type of behavior is okay just shows our complete lack of etiquette and regard for others. If it's necessary to minimize others in order to elevate ourselves, then it's obvious that we're not as important as we pretend to be.

It's crazy how regular people can make themselves celebrities every day. It's even crazier what constitutes a celebrity in the eyes of the public. Nowadays, a celebrity seems to be any random self-proclaimed influencer, trending TikTok performer, or reality show cast member. Why are they being celebrated? What puts them in the same class as award-winning actors, singers, and athletes? At least, the celebrities of yesteryear used to earn their status in entertainment by having actual talent.

Many of today's celebrities are appointing themselves a sobriquet of royalty as part of yet another cringe-inducing trend. Some are even delusional enough to regard themselves as gods. They place imperious demands on their fans and the media to brownnose them because simply being famous, being wealthy, and living their dream is not enough. What's pathetic is the desperation of celebrities clout chasing when they already have clout. What they don't understand is that no one person can truthfully call themselves the king or queen of anything, it's the people who decide.

Why are the American people so obsessed with the British monarchy? He's not our king, and she wasn't our queen. I don't believe in royalty. I don't think that anyone should bow before another. No one is born with "blue blood," and regality is not hereditary. What would make any human entity believe that they possess the "divine right" of royalty? I don't understand why we make these people greater than they are or greater than we are. They're human! We all bleed the same.

The world is rife with sycophantic stans who live vicariously through their idols. They seem to get their sense of self-worth based on how well that celebrity is doing. They over-stream and over-purchase that celebrity's music, movies, and merchandise to further elevate them. Stan culture has gotten disturbingly obsessive. At any given time, you can find psychotic fandoms incessantly praising and defending their celebrity heroes on social media. It's not a stretch to think that these fanatics would kill—even die—for these celebrities.

Obsession is being controlled by demons externally. Why would we allow ourselves to be controlled by our preoccupation with celebrities? Why are we so consumed with people we don't even know? I don't applaud celebrity, and I don't condone idolatry. To worship an idol is utterly idle. The worth of a life is the soul, not the title. It's obvious that many of us live vicariously through celebrities because we lack self-esteem. Perhaps we wouldn't be so drawn to the asterism if we valued ourselves as much as we do them.

## *Culture of Arrogance: When Humans Lose Humanity*

In today's world, humility seems to be antiquated. Arrogance is overrated, but is often exhibited because it's more entertaining than humility and, therefore, gets more attention. It's become so trendy to be boastful and self-aggrandizing that most people don't hesitate to create false claims of accomplishments just for a flex.

Insecurity hides behind arrogance hoping to fool its observers. Arrogant people go out of their way to convince you of their greatness because they need your conviction to convince themselves. Because they're insecure, they don't feel like their opinion is valid unless someone else believes it. Too many people are convinced that they can cover up insecurity with arrogance.

What annoys me about arrogant people is that they can never seem to own up to their arrogance. Instead, they excuse their comportment with a safer word like *confidence*. By definition, an arrogant person should at least be bold enough to acknowledge their arrogance without backing away from the stigma to which it's attached.

Arrogance is entitlement that expects privilege. A lot of spoiled, wealthy socialites with "entertaining" personalities have been given their own reality shows simply because our culture has a careless way of rewarding bad behavior. This practice is a form of villain glorification, which I believe played a big role in the election of Trump. The villain can be seen as the underdog—which people like to root for—only more entertaining due to their reckless irreverence.

The culture of arrogance is clearly manifested in the obsessive world of college sports, primarily football and basketball. These student athletes are taught that sports is of paramount importance, even above academics. Their schools treat them like celebrities, and they learn to be held to an alternate standard than the rest of the student body. This special treatment creates and encourages an arrogance that gives them a false sense of superiority. We've all seen and heard countless news stories about college sports scandals including sexual assaults, cover-ups, academic fraud, illegal recruiting, and bribery. These people know that they can quite literally get away with murder; thus, their arrogance.

Most bloggers and critics have an arrogant audacity. They seem to view their own opinions as facts, and criminally overestimate the importance of those opinions. Because of their self-perceived infinite social reach, they believe that they have the power to make or break a person or business. Needless to say, they make capital of this influence at every chance.

Much like bloggers and critics, many journalists and news anchors seem to possess an exaggerated sense of self-importance. They often twist serious stories with needless embellishments just to make them more entertaining. They feign sympathy for the subjects of these stories, even after callously lusting for the opportunity to exploit them. It's all about getting the story, and the worse a story is, the better. It doesn't matter who they take advantage of or offend in the process. Anything that will boost their egos or win them awards is fair game. What they never seem to understand is that they didn't invent the news, they just report it.

What are we afraid to lose by being humble and showing compassion? When did humanity stop being human? It's odd how most of society views confidence. They see it as never having self-doubt, and valuing pretense. What they don't see is that there's confidence in admitting your insecurity. It's time to exchange pretense for modesty, and be strong enough to be real.

## *Second-Sex Citizens: The Perpetual War of Feminism*

If men were as virile and confident as we portray ourselves to be, then more of us would be feminists. A masculine feminist is secure and open-minded enough to support the cause of feminism, which fights for the equal rights of the sexes. Only a weak man requires that a woman be obsequiously submissive in order to maintain his power.

Americans are the patriots of a patriarchy—a nation shaped by the "Founding Fathers." We're a country deeply rooted in toxic masculinity and chauvinism. From the antiquated traditions of the deep south—which require women to be subservient housewives who do nothing more than cook, clean, and caretake—to modern day corporate practices—which keep women out of positions of power and making less money than their male counterparts—misogyny is a part of the American way. There are a lot of weak men who hate all women because one woman hurt their feelings. These men dedicate their lives to making women pay to restore their wounded egos.

Women are routinely subjected to verbal and sexual harassment not only in the workplace, but in every place occupied by men. They're like prey on the bottom of the gender food chain and are literally up for grabs. Women often feel too powerless and voiceless to defend themselves, so they remain silent and learn to accept it. They're objectified reflexively and degraded with monikers like "baby," "sweetie," "honey," and "bitch." Somehow, women seem to be innately acclimated to sexism. They're so accustomed to it that some of them often don't recognize it, yet they're also conditioned to make excuses for a man's sexism to downplay how serious it is.

Female human beings are not only burdened by menses and childbirth, they're too often left to care for their offspring without the help of the father. They're forced into marriage as children. They're also sold into sex trafficking as children. Women are abused in every possible way; mentally, emotionally, physically, even spiritually. They're beaten, they're drugged, they're raped, they're controlled. On top of that, they're pressured with impossible physical standards. The strength of a woman is unfathomable, yet so is the way that we treat them. The life of the fairer sex is anything but fair.

In many countries—including America—more value is placed on male births than female births. This is evident with the popularity of gender-reveal videos, which often show a clear bias in favor of blue over pink. You can see many soon-to-be fathers and soon-to-be brothers, uncles, etc. expressing their shameless disappointment at the sight of the color pink, with some even shedding tears.

Somehow, the privileged White man—who holds all of the power in America—has made himself the number one victim in this country. With the #MeToo and Black Lives Matter movements, and the growing push for social justice, many White men feel threatened by the possibility of equality. They whine about how their opinions are always misconstrued as racist or sexist, and how they're generally under attack. It's fascinating to see the histrionics they exhibit out of fear of losing the power to suppress women with their White male supremacy.

During the inauguration of Donald Trump, hundreds of thousands of women gathered to protest. His election represented—in part—an attack on gender equality, civil rights, and women's reproductive rights. Meanwhile, with the Supreme Court overturning Roe v. Wade, women are losing the rights to their own bodies. Why is it that so many old, White men have the power to force a woman who was raped and impregnated by her father to give birth to his child? Soon, they'll find a way to convict women for their miscarriages. It's been said that if men could get pregnant, there would be birth control available at every turn.

Instead of regressing back to the 1950s, there should be more laws that support women—especially Black women who are probably the most discriminated against and least protected demographic in America. Women should have the right to be women in all spaces without being subjected to harassment or criticism—It's pitiful how some people still take offense to women breastfeeding in public.

We were all birthed from a woman. Our mothers, daughters, sisters, aunts, and grandmothers are women, so—as men—why wouldn't we hold women in the highest regard? As the bearers of human life, women should be uplifted to the heights of queendom and not blocked or limited by the male ego. This glass ceiling will exist for as long as we allow it to exist. Buildings made with glass ceilings are susceptible to stones. Therefore, gender equality is just a stone's throw away.

## *Earth Reset: The Coronavirus Pandemic*

On March 11, 2020, the world shut down. The lights turned off, the signs went up, and everything changed forever. A pandemic was declared, unlike any health crisis we've experienced in our lifetime. It felt like the end of the world—an extinction level event. Suddenly, cities turned into ghost towns, we were forced into quarantine and social distancing, and we realized that nothing was ever going to be the same again.

The days and weeks that followed were marked by fear and anxiety. We remained glued to the news to try to understand what this virus was doing to the world, which only heightened our anxiety. We began selfishly hoarding toilet paper and other supplies as we prepared to remain in a state of indefinite lockdown. The news and media relentlessly repeated the same buzz words and phrases to underscore "the new normal" during these "unprecedented" and "uncertain times." With every new Covid case and every new Covid death, there seemed to be a minute-by-minute reminder of each "grim milestone."

The quarantine effort proved to be a failure, and summer 2020 was cancelled. The trauma of this pandemic left many of us with depression, stress, and insomnia to go with our anxiety. A lot of people turned to drugs and other vices to cope. People seemed to suffer from a pandemic-fueled mental illness that gave rise to hostility and violence. The pandemic exacerbated the worst qualities of most people. Fed up with mask mandates and ready for an economic restart, many people began to rally and protest. Though Covid was still very much a threat, they ignored mask and social distancing requirements with selfish defiance. There were also mask Karens who started fights with people who had the gall to wear a mask, even coughing on them to exploit their fear.

With the economy in recession, many people put money over health in fighting to reopen the country—even with new Covid variants popping up regularly like storm systems during hurricane season (Hurricane Delta, Hurricane Omicron). This premature reopening led to a second wave of Covid cases. With all of the emotional and physical suffering it inflicted, we still insisted on politicizing a pandemic. Ridiculously, if you were a Conservative, you had to be anti-mask and anti-vax. You also had to believe that Covid didn't exist anymore or that it never existed at all. Unfortunately, pretending that this virus didn't exist didn't make it go away.

Former game show host and Trump enthusiast Chuck Woolery famously tweeted that "Everyone is lying" about Covid-19—"The CDC, media, Democrats, our doctors." The following day, he tweeted that his son tested positive for the virus. Under Trump's reckless leadership, many Conservatives spread dangerous misinformation about the virus and its vaccine. They continue to have an illogical mistrust of science and health experts. There are hypocrites who believe in "My body, my choice" when it comes to getting the vaccine, but reject the same theory when it comes to abortion rights.

There are many people whose pride makes them assume that their body is strong enough to fight off the virus should they acquire it. They foolishly feel that getting vaccinated makes them look scared or weak. With more and more companies enforcing vaccine mandates as a basis of employment, the country remains divided on the issue. On one hand, I believe that employees who occupied their positions pre-pandemic shouldn't be forced to get vaccinated if they oppose, and—on the other hand—I believe that employers have a right and a duty to maintain a safe and healthy workplace. Still, the vaccine opposition seems very conditional. It's funny how everyone wanted the vaccine when it was exclusive.

Despite the tragedies and the trauma of the pandemic, there were many silver linings. Everyone in the entire world was going through the same thing, which collectively brought us closer together in spirit. We were all forced to stop and refocus our lives, prioritizing the things that matter most. Many of us rearranged our work lives, whether that meant working from home to spend more time with our families or joining the Great Resignation in leaving our jobs to pursue our passion. Our essential workers were finally valued for what they do as we learned to spread love to each other. We learned a lot about ourselves, and many of us grew from this experience.

So what was the reason for this pandemic? Was it God's test, or was it His scourge for our sins? It feels like a means for our atonement. If nothing else, it's a reminder of how fragile life is, and that we must serve our purpose while we still have time. Perhaps Earth just hit the reset button. It seems to have a way of self-cleaning like an oven.

# CHAPTER 2 - RACE & DIVERSITY



### *The Glass Closet: Racism Hidden in Plain Sight*

Race is a social construct created for the purpose of division. Racism is a result of that division. Is it possible that we're all subconsciously racist? Are some of us just ignorant to our own racist ideals? I'm sure that we're all guilty of a little "light-hearted" racism, which includes racist jokes and stereotypes that seem to be generally acceptable. However, it's still racism, and racism is always wrong. Subconsciously, we know it's wrong; that's why we make such an effort to conceal it or make excuses for it. Some people like to call it an "unconscious bias" to sugarcoat their very conscious prejudice.

The most American thing about our country is racism. It's embedded in our history, and it's typical in our culture. As terrible as it is, it's a reality that we've all come to expect, and too many of us are okay with it. Racism is so American that when I see an American flag waving proudly on the porch of a house or on the back of a pickup truck, my first thought is racist suspicion. I instantly assume that the house or the pickup truck belongs to someone who is White and loves America because—in every way possible—it's *their* country. The American flag is starting to look like a Confederate flag—a symbol of hate.

Social media magnifies and perpetuates racism. It's where bigots come out of the woodwork to say—or type—what they would never say to the subject's face. It seems like almost every other week, some well-known person makes an offensive or racist comment on social media, which they end up deleting, and for which they later apologize. If this is a free country with freedom of speech, then why be apologetic for how you feel? Why make excuses and backtrack? Why tweet and delete? Cowardice. So many bigoted cowards are bold enough to be racist, but not bold enough to admit that they're racist.

Nobody's racist ... until they get upset. Quite often, when a White person is angry with a Black person, they love to keep their finger on the "nigger" trigger. It's the biggest, most accessible weapon in their arsenal. What's really troubling is their attempt to normalize the word *nigger*—"If Black people say it, then why can't we?" They seem to view Black people's use of this word as some sort of Black privilege. Ignorance can never grasp the fact that this is a deplorable word no matter who uses it or the context in which they do. Those who claim that *nigger* isn't in their vocabulary can be just as hypocritical. Why is it necessary for them to actually say the word when explaining how they don't say it?

Many White people throw the word *nigger* around casually among their friends and relatives to intentionally degrade Black people, so I don't understand why they apologize for doing so since they already know how offensive it is before saying it. These insincere apologies only come about when someone is caught spewing this hatred, especially when it's potentially damaging to their career. They always apologize for making a "mistake," when they actually made a *choice*. The mistake was *choosing* to say what they said. For all of the racist toxins they spit into the air, it's unbearable to them to be branded a racist. They defend themselves against this truth with every ounce of their being. It's funny how they're more comfortable with the word *nigger* than the word *racist*.

There are White people who have a sick obsession with Black people that takes the form of racist fetishism. There are White men who date—and even marry—Black women with low self-esteem specifically to fulfill their twisted fantasy of grooming them to be their slaves. Disturbed bigots like these are convinced that they can conceal their racism by having Black people in their lives or—in other words—by keeping their enemies closer. Many White people make sure to have a token Black friend to excuse their racism. They figure that if one Black person is okay with it, then it's fine. They use these Black people as walking props to show society that "some of my best friends are Black."

There are also White people who adopt Black children and keep them secluded from Black culture and Black history. Too many of them want to be the "great White hope" who saves Black children from Blackness. They convince themselves that they're doing God's work by bringing poor Black people into the privileged White world, but using us as charity is always for *their* benefit—as evidenced by the family portrayed in the film *The Blind Side*. People who have this White savior complex exploit Black people under the guise of altruism to make themselves feel less prejudiced. However, it doesn't work that way. Having a relationship or an association with someone of a different race does not exempt you from being a racist.

Many people know that Thomas Jefferson was a slave master who fathered children with the enslaved Sally Hemings. He is highly regarded as a former president and advocate for the emancipation of slaves, even though he owned hundreds of slaves during his lifetime. Slave trader Zephaniah Kingsley Jr. is regarded for having been a "liberal" slave owner who extended leniency to those whom he enslaved. He fathered eleven children with multiple Black women, but encouraged his children to have White spouses. He declared that Black people were "superior" to White people "physically and morally," yet he kept them enslaved. Ignorant people like he and Jefferson claim to oppose racism while having no idea that they are in fact racist.

In May 2018, actress/comedienne Roseanne Barr was compelled to tweet a thoughtless remark about former senior advisor to President Obama Valerie Jarrett in which she compared Jarrett to an ape. As a somewhat shocking result, the ABC network took action by cancelling Barr's number-one-rated sitcom and not turning a blind eye to racist hate-speech in favor of corporate gain. Barr apologized and emphasized that she is not a racist, but her intention with that original tweet was clear: She wanted to gain social media attention by making a controversial, irreverent "joke." What she didn't expect was to be held accountable for her actions. She let her hatred of another person—and her need to spread that negativity to millions of followers—cost her not only a job, but the respect of so many people, which severely damaged her legacy. It's true that we don't have to agree with each other, but why do we allow that to escalate to hateful behavior?

In March 2016, Joe's Crab Shack made headlines with one of their Minneapolis restaurants for using place mats that depicted the lynching of two Black men. Of course, the higher-ups of the company issued a damage-control apology, but how could they have overlooked this revolting display of racism in the first place? How can the American majority be so blind and desensitized to racism? Too many of them don't think that this type of behavior is a big deal. They seem to want us to be offended and get upset about it so that they can complain about how sensitive we are, or maybe they're just appealing to their target demographic.

Racism has also made its way into the mass marketing of major fashion/apparel brands. There are many Italian brands—including Gucci, Prada, and Dolce & Gabbana—that have used Blackface on their merchandise. In January 2018, H&M received substantial backlash for an image on their website that showed a young Black boy in a hooded sweatshirt which contained the phrase, "Coolest monkey in the jungle." About two weeks later, Amazon came under fire for merchandise they sold which contained the phrase, "Slavery gets shit done." Only in a despicably racist world could slogans like these be used to sell product. The fact that these ideas didn't cause concern for anyone on the marketing/production teams of these companies before they were advertised—and later apologized for—speaks volumes to my previous statement.

Styles of music, fashion, etc. are often categorized as "urban," which we all know is just code for "Black." The majority of White people seem to have gotten comfortable with denoting Black people with coded language. The term "African American" is a lousy attempt at political correctness and merely a means of titular segregation. If Black people are considered African American, shouldn't White people be referred to as European Americans? In a general context, the term doesn't even make sense because not all Black people are African American. Also, there are many White Americans with North and South African roots who would never be labeled as African American. This just goes to show how White America finds it necessary to categorize Black people and reduce our citizenship to only half American. If we were born in America, why does an asterisk have to be put on our nationality?

There are constant attempts to marginalize Black people. Many White people want to get rid of the BET network, the NAACP, and Black History Month. Some have even argued that there should be a White Entertainment Television network since Black people have BET. What they conveniently fail to realize is that *every* major television network is basically White entertainment television with White people—as reflected in society—making up a vast majority of TV characters. Black people and other minorities have been forced to create our own networks just to be fairly represented on television. What many people also don't understand is the overall idea of niche television with networks that market to specific demographics, e.g., Hispanic people, queer people, women, sports enthusiasts, Christians, scholars, etc. If we eliminate BET and Black History Month for not being "all-inclusive," should we also get rid of CMT and Christmas?

In 2018, a high school wrestler was forced by a bigoted referee to have his dreadlocks cut off on the gym floor right before his match. Like every other racist institution in America, the intent was to strip this young man of not only his Blackness, but his dignity—just like they stripped us of our culture when they kidnapped our ancestors and shipped them here from Africa. In 2023, yet another young Black man was punished for having dreadlocks as his Texas high school suspended him and banished him to a temporary alternative school. The school also made a point to enforce the suspension a day before the state's CROWN Act—an anti-discrimination law based on hair style and texture—went into effect. These institutions are willing to go to extreme measures to force us to assimilate to a White world—to control, in addition to what's accessible to us, how we look. As ridiculous as it is for us to be discriminated against for our hair, it's sad to see anti-Blackness normalized and regulated. Somehow, being Black is no longer a civil right.

In April 2021, Republican senator Tim Scott and America's first Black Vice President Kamala Harris both proclaimed that "America isn't a racist country." Scott—having grown up a Black male in South Carolina, and today being dubbed "Uncle Tim"—is well aware of the racism that exists in this country. Harris—in a desperate attempt at bipartisanship—agreed with his statement, and thereby exempted the GOP from addressing or resolving the racism to which they regularly contribute. Not only is it sad to see two Black leaders preach this absurdity, it's also dangerous. To be willfully blind to racism means that nothing has to be done to change the system of racist actions we see and hear about every single day.

The issuance of government aid during a major crisis in the United States seems to be contingent upon the socioeconomic status of any particular area. It's no secret that President Bush handled the relief efforts after Hurricane Katrina very poorly, and it's no coincidence that most of the devastation took place in the low-income, predominantly Black areas of New Orleans. During the Chicago heat wave of 1995, over 700 mostly-Black and impoverished residents suffered heat-related deaths. The death toll was so immense—and grew so fast—that hundreds of bodies were stored in refrigerated trucks like expired meat product, while others were thrown in a mass grave. Still, leaders and politicians carelessly denied the magnitude of this disaster; authorities were slow to even recognize it.

Residents in areas like Africatown, AL have to deal with cancer-causing industrial pollution and land and water-contaminating toxic waste simply because of their "zip code." For decades, many urban communities in this country have had to deal with poisonous lead in their drinking water. A public health state of emergency was issued in 2016 in Flint, MI when it was discovered that their water supply had been contaminated. Apparently, Michigan Governor Rick Snyder chose to save money by experimenting with a water supply change at the expense of Flint's impoverished minority residents. The Flint Water Crisis—like others before and after—has led to speculation that the government is purposely poisoning the drinking water in Black communities. Catastrophes like these are given the typical nonchalant response due to environmental racism and implicit bias.

The word *ghetto* is thrown around by many White people as an adjective to describe substandard things, including Black people. There's a general misconception that Black people are the only occupants of America's impoverished communities, but the ghetto is not reserved exclusively for Black people. Those who use this word in such a way should realize that the ghetto is a real place with real struggle and oppression, and when they use it to devalue things, it's an insult to those who have to live in this undesirable setting. Inner city neighborhoods are littered with corner stores and liquor stores that sell alcohol, tobacco, narcotics, and unhealthy foods to people of color. Merchants even market some of these products specifically to those in the inner city, e.g., rappers on bags of potato chips.

Racist politicians and journalists use the worst members of our community as representation for all Black people, making unfair generalizations of what they've called a "deteriorating Black culture." There's a stigma on Black names, Blackness, and merely the word *black*. The term *negrophobia* has made its way into the cultural lexicon in the midst of all of the cases of police brutality. Some have tried to blame negrophobia—an irrational fear of Black people—on these incidents. However, I believe that lending relevance to such a word is only an ignorant attempt to justify the hateful injustices it causes. It's true that hate is based on fear, but using a word to explain or excuse the racist behavior of adults who have the ability to determine right from wrong just seems insulting and completely unnecessary.

Because of the coronavirus pandemic and the racist language of Donald Trump, Meghan McCain, and other Conservatives who called it the "China virus" or the "Chinese virus," there were a slew of hate crimes targeting the Asian American community. Many videos emerged of people attacking elderly members of this community, and—in yet another act of White terrorism—Robert Aaron Long shot and killed eight people at multiple massage parlors in Atlanta, including six women of Asian descent. It's become very "American" for so-called leaders like Trump to lead by a prejudiced example. When they teach us how to hate, it gives license to racism. When they teach us whom to hate, people of color always seem to lose their lives.

Why is it that when famous people of color embrace their culture, they're said to have a political agenda? From what I've observed, when you're a Black person who achieves a certain level of power and wealth, there are some White people who don't like to be reminded that you're Black. Anything that we do to empower ourselves just to be seen as equal is taken as a threat to White supremacy. Simply taking pride in our culture solicits a negative reaction from White people that's reminiscent of the slave master's fear of an insurrection. Being pro-Black does not mean being anti-White, just like being against police brutality does not mean being anti-police.

Black athletes being drafted and traded draws unsettling parallels to slavery. They're conditioned physically and mentally to be prize-winning show ponies for rich White men. These White men build their wealth from the labor of these athletes much like they did with slaves. Southern country clubs used to hire Black men exclusively for service roles just for the opportunity to degrade them. Many White men seem to have an obsessive and pathetic need to feel superior. If there were ever a situation where Black people made up a vast majority in a field of corporate, political, or societal power, it would be absolutely unacceptable to most White people because it deviates so sharply from the expected norm.

In April 2016, it was announced that abolitionist leader Harriet Tubman would replace President Andrew Jackson on the front of the $20 bill. The response to this historical achievement mimicked the racial divide of our country. Many Conservatives were—for no good reason—completely against this change. Donald Trump and Ben Carson both stated that Tubman should be on the $2 bill instead. What makes a Black woman who led hundreds of slaves to freedom less worthy than a White former president who owned slaves?

Many White people make a point to mention President Abraham Lincoln during Black History Month to slight Black achievements. The implication is that Black people owe every privilege we have to the White man. Lincoln is often referenced as the singular reason for our freedom; however, abolishing slavery didn't eliminate his propensity for racism. Lincoln once said, "I am not, nor ever have been in favor of making voters or jurors of negroes, nor of qualifying them to hold office, nor intermarry with White people."

After the election of President Barack Obama, it was said that we live in a post-racial society. Even with all of the despicable acts of hate that have occurred since, we seem surprised that racism still exists. It is my sincere belief that racism will, unfortunately, always exist. There will be moments when it will rise to unthinkable heights, and seasons when it will quell to almost tolerable levels. Shamefully, new generations of racists continue to be bred thanks to ignorant, neglectful parents who intentionally brainwash hate into the minds of their innocent children.

As long as there are different races, there will be racism. People need division because we live for competition. We have a pitiful need to cast an indictment on who's inferior, inept, and incompetent. Racism is a disease of insecurity. Racism is for the weak. What should be completely obvious by now is that hateful people are miserable. There's no way that you can be so consumed with mongering hate and still be happy with yourself. When you devote your existence to hatred toward other races, you give them exactly what you don't want them to have: power. Having the capacity to hate is *your* problem and it only minimizes *you*, not the object of your hate.

It's time to stop playing dumb and denying this glass-closeted racism. We all see it and contribute to it, so we know that it exists. We can't continue disguising it as an unconscious bias because it's a conscious prejudice. We can't keep pretending to be unaware of racism because we've lived long enough to know better. We're too evolved as humans to still be in this mindset. At some point, we have to take accountability. Those of us who choose not to be blind to racism will be the eyes of the ignorant. Hey, racism: We see you, and we're going to keep calling you out.

## *Carte Blanche: Playing the "White Card" of White Privilege*

In America—like every other place in the world—being White is the passport to privilege. White privilege is inherent, so many White people aren't even aware that they have it. It's so inherent, it's an entitlement—an expectation of exclusive accessibility. Possession of the "White card" gives them *carte blanche* to do, be, or have pretty much anything they want. Being White is the definition of freedom as it was only intended for them. Collectively, I believe that White people will always have a privileged mentality because everything that they see and hear in America tells them that they're superior.

White privilege is easily defined by a double standard which insists that White people can do, say, and get away with things that Black people—and other minorities—cannot. It's an unfair advantage that White people give themselves and we—often unknowingly—give them as well. White people can patronize country clubs, take over public spaces, be arrogant and boastful, curse and be loud in public, fight with police, resist arrest, display racist insignia, carry guns, be aggressive and hostile, demand justice, etc., but when the rest of us do the same, it's unacceptable. As Black people, we're always expected to be secondary—even tertiary—never equal, and racism is the way of keeping us in our place. There will always be White people who utilize every opportunity to assert their sense of authority over us.

As White people play the White card, Black people are *black*listed. For Black people, our race plays a part in almost everything that we do, say, and think. This is an issue that White people will never have, as evidenced by their White privilege. To be able to simply *be* without constantly being persecuted for your race is the greatest privilege known to man, and it's clear that such a privilege is only reserved for one group of people. White privilege encompasses opportunities, passes, and the comfort with which they get to live their lives. They have an intrinsic advantage with employment, housing, education, etc. Because they represent a global majority, they have the privilege of power. There are many areas in Africa where Black people are the majority, yet White people are still in power. Somehow, White privilege justifies White supremacy.

In an infamous 1971 interview with *Playboy* magazine, America's cowboy hero John Wayne said "I believe in White supremacy," a fact which I'm sure he asserted upon his three Hispanic wives. He said that Black people were not "educated to a point of responsibility," and, therefore, unworthy of "leadership." Meanwhile, in the good ol' U-S-of-A—a land that he said was rightfully taken "away from the Indians"—there was an airport named in his honor, and he was awarded the Presidential Medal of Freedom. An enduring icon of White supremacy, Wayne is celebrated as much for his bigotry as his career accomplishments.

There are shrines to White supremacy all over the United States. Mount Rushmore—while a stunning achievement in sculpture—is just another Confederate monument. It honors presidents who owned slaves, destroyed Native settlements, and ordered the executions of Native people. It remains a constant, prominent, taunting reminder to Native Americans of their genocide and stolen land. Its sculptor, Gutzon Borglum, was a supporter of the Ku Klux Klan who was also involved in the carving of Stone Mountain, the Mount Rushmore of the KKK.

In America, racism is a "tradition." What we see today stems from the deep-seated racism of the deep south. It's unbelievable how badly they want to preserve and perpetuate this tradition of racism. They preach a Confederate rhetoric while waving their Confederate flags. These flags are emblazoned with the Confederate cross, which is basically the American swastika. William Thompson—who created the design and symbolic purpose of what would later become the Confederate flag—was quoted in the book *Our Flag*, by George Preble saying, "As a people, we are fighting to maintain the heavenly ordained supremacy of the White man over the inferior or colored race." He called it the "White man's flag." Supporters of today's Confederate flag argue that it's actually a "rebel flag" that represents Southern pride. The *rebel* aspect of this flag seems to suggest, "We won't conform to the wishes of those against whom we're prejudiced." To proudly display this flag while being fully aware of the racist history behind it doesn't make you an "accidental racist," it makes you a deliberate one.

Not many people are going to admit to being racist because it's financially detrimental. When White celebrities are outed for their racist actions, they suddenly want to be educated about racism to clean up their image for the sake of their career. Actor Mark Wahlberg was emboldened to believe that he could be granted a pardon to erase his racist past. It seems that he wanted to go back in time and whitewash all of the violent, racist assaults he issued to Asian men and Black children in the late '80s. In February 2021, country singer Morgan Wallen was caught on camera calling his friend a "pussy ass nigga" multiple times. His record label immediately suspended him, his songs were removed from country radio, and he issued the standard insincere apology in which he vowed to do better. Nevertheless, his record sales increased significantly, and his album remained at number one on the Billboard 200 for weeks following the incident.

Similarly in 2018, Brewers pitcher Josh Hader was under fire when his old racist and homophobic tweets resurfaced. He also apologized and blamed his youth and immaturity at the time for his tweets. In his next home game following the incident, he received a standing ovation. These fans weren't cheering a soldier returning home from war, they were proudly and defiantly supporting disgusting behavior. Even if he and Wallen aren't racist, their fans clearly are. It's crazy how so many White people defend and support racism, but can't admit that they're racist.

It's not enough for some White people to make racist remarks, they want Black people to be okay with it too. They take offense to us being offended by the offensive things that they say. Some of them actually get upset when we don't buy their lazy attempts to veil their racism; others say, "It's not as bad as it used to be." Does that mean that we should just accept it? Imagine the arrogant, self-authorized audacity of a White person defending their right to use the word *nigger* and still expecting not to be seen as racist. In case it isn't obvious, this is White privilege.

Vaudeville entertainer Al Jolson is regarded by critics as the "king of blackface." White performers have used blackface to mock Black people for having the culture, style, and swag that they attempt to embody. I've never understood how they could simultaneously detest, adore, envy, and obsess over us. Jolson is hailed by White historians as a White savior who opened doors for Black actors. They are always quick to mention the few Black people who were blind to his use of blackface and considered him to be an inspiration. This man portrayed and perpetuated insanely offensive Black stereotypes under the purported guise of metaphorical racial suffering. These White historians inadvertently highlight his White privilege by making him the voice—and face—of the disenfranchised Negroes of his time. Jolson exploited and demeaned Black people and was given undue credit for making our music and culture acceptable, but because White historians have rewritten his intentions and have given him cultural significance, I guess we should just ignore his shameless degradation of the Black race.

It's frustrating when White people say that they "don't see color" because—whether we want to or not—we *all* see color. It's also frustrating when they say "we're all the same" because we're certainly not treated as if we're all the same. We don't suffer the same injustices, and we don't have the same privileges. When they say things like this, it just comes off as an attempt to wash over the fact that racism and prejudice exist. It's obvious that some White people don't want us to think that racism exists because it benefits them. For some reason, they expect us to just get over it and adopt their delusional ignorance, even making it a point to tell us how we should feel. The same White people who complain about Black people playing the race card secretly love when we do because it gives them an excuse to turn their issues back on us. It gives them a reason to claim that we're playing the victim or making excuses. White people invented racism, but they hate when we acknowledge their work. When we play the "race card," we're only playing the hand that we were dealt.

I recently was made aware of the term "reverse racism." It attempts to define the perceived racism against White people by Black people and other minorities who are usually the victims of *their* racism. It seems like they want to be the oppressed ones so that they can be entitled to complain. It amazes me how White privilege still needs something to complain about, and it's ironic how these racists don't like to acknowledge their White privilege. I believe that Black people are inherently born as counter-racists. The history in our bloodline tells us that White people will automatically hate us and see us as inferior. Innately, we react to this presumption by expecting racism until shown otherwise.

A lot of White people would rather ignore issues of racism just because it makes them uncomfortable. Their White privilege doesn't allow them to understand that Black people have to live with the discomfort of racism every day of our lives. It's startling that even in this day and age, some people are still too comfortable and ignorant to see what the big deal is. When it comes to the history of slavery, they say that we should just "get over it;" however, when it comes to 9/11, Pearl Harbor, and every White man's war, we must "never forget." They often dismiss racism by saying, "Well, it's never happened to me," or "I've never seen it." As Black people, we simply want White people to understand that this is *our* experience, and that they should just hear us instead of centerizing our issues.

Many White people—as self-perceived *true* Americans—strongly insist that all other races in America celebrate their patriotic holidays without question or complaint. They oppose the rights of Black people who choose not to celebrate Independence Day, even though Black people were anything but free in 1776 when the Declaration of Independence was created. The Declaration states that "all men are created equal," even though it was drafted by privileged White men who owned slaves. They also expect us to honor Christopher Columbus—a known slave trader and colonizer—and to worship *their* forefathers as the forefathers of this country.

White privilege has created a stupefying double standard which contends that something is good when White people do it, and bad when Black people do. When White University of Iowa basketball star Caitlin Clark taunted her opponents with arrogant gestures and trash-talk, she was called "competitive" and a "role model." When Black Louisiana State University basketball star Angel Reese displayed the same behavior, she was called "classless," among other racially-motivated epithets. When the mostly-Black LSU women's basketball team won the 2023 NCAA title that's traditionally accompanied with a visit to the White House, first lady Jill Biden suggested that the mostly-White runner-up Iowa team be invited as well. Not only do Black people have to work twice as hard as White people to get the same recognition, our accomplishments are also minimized when they're seen as taking away from those of the privileged race.

Racist taunting from spectators is often overlooked or dismissed as a normal part of sports culture. However, only non-White athletes seem to be the targeted victims of these attacks. There have been many instances of Black soccer and hockey players having bananas thrown at them in addition to the racial slurs that Black athletes commonly receive. It's a shame how much racist verbal abuse Jeremy Lin had to endure from basketball fans, fellow players, and the media just for having the audacity to be a great athlete while also being Asian American.

Black people—and other people of color—deal with so many microaggressions from White people on a daily basis. Of course these comments and actions are never *intended* to be racist, no matter how stereotypical they are. They seem to serve as slightly watered-down epithets that allow ignorant people to insult us without our supposed knowing. In the workplace, we're expected to be the token ambassadors for all things "Black." We're required to speak on behalf of all other Black people and to represent them at all times. As problematic and infuriating as it is, we simply aren't seen as individuals. If one of us is "bad," then we all are. Every day, so many of us have to deal with being harassed, kicked out of facilities, and even arrested for disturbing the peace with our silent Blackness.

In April of 2018, two Black men were arrested at a Philadelphia Starbucks simply for sitting and waiting to meet with their friend. The politically-phrased "unconscious bias" that prompted the White Starbucks manager to call the police on these two Black men led the CEO of the company to conduct "racial-bias training" for all employees. Since then, there have been several meme-worthy incidents in which White people call the police on Black people for barbecuing in the park, selling bottled water, using a swimming pool, and for daring to have fun and enjoy their lives comfortably.

Sadly, White privilege extends to the mostly-White law enforcement here in America. Knowing that the system is set up to defend and protect them, many White people take full advantage of it. They are well aware of the unspoken law that allows them to claim that they "feared for their lives" after shooting and killing a Black person. This same hateful energy compels them to call the cops on innocent Black people who commit the crime of being in *their* social space. Not only are they well aware of the privilege they have, they're completely apathetic about the dangerous consequences that privilege has for Black people.

In 2017, Carolyn Bryant Donham confessed to lying about a Black teenager named Emmett Till flirting with her, for which he was gruesomely beaten and killed by White supremacists in 1955. In 1923, Fannie Taylor lied about being assaulted by a Black man in order to hide the fact that she was beaten by a White man with whom she was having an affair. This thoughtless, racist lie created the Rosewood massacre that claimed countless lives and left a Black town burned to the ground. White women have weaponized their feminine Whiteness against Black men for ages. Since these White women represent a majority *and* a minority, they get to be the oppressor and the victim at their convenience.

White privilege is a cruelly unfair reality that has had tragic repercussions for people of color. As the majority, White people have representation everywhere that Black people don't. This is the basis for White privilege, White supremacy, and systemic racism. White people will always have the privilege of not having to worry about their race being a barrier for corporate, educational, societal, or economic advancement. The White card is never declined.

## *Retribution: The Black Lives Matter Movement*

Say their names: George Floyd, Breonna Taylor, Ahmaud Arbery, Daunte Wright, Ma'Khia Bryant, Michael Brown, Eric Garner, Tamir Rice, Walter Scott, Alton Sterling, Philando Castile, Stephon Clark, Trayvon Martin ..., an endless, ever-growing list of Black lives taken by the hands of White supremacy.

Colin Kaepernick took a knee in protest of the injustices of evil, bigoted cops. An evil, bigoted coward took a knee on the neck of George Floyd. For eight minutes and forty-six seconds, this monster took out his racist resentment toward Black lives by ending one. This thoughtless tragedy was made public through the constant, desensitized replaying of a video in which we see a Black man being tortured to death by a first responder. It's sad to think that if this lynching hadn't been recorded—if it hadn't incited a firestorm across the country and overseas—the killer in uniform would have gone free.

There is no safe place to be Black in America. Being Black in America is a death sentence. Many White people and members of law enforcement are anesthetized to the loss of Black lives, which they see as having no value. Many of our young Black boys are afraid of being seen in public by police. There was a heartbreaking video that went viral in 2020, which shows a young Black boy playing basketball alone in his driveway when a police car turned down his block. Even though this child had done absolutely nothing wrong, he felt the need to hide behind his parents' vehicle until the cops drove past. Because of the senseless actions of law enforcement in America, innocent Black children—who should have no worries—are in fear for their lives.

The phrase "Black lives matter" is upsetting to many White people because they simply don't agree with it. They despise the fact that many people feel that Black lives do matter, and they don't want to be reminded of that. They hate all of the attention that the Black Lives Matter movement receives because they want that attention for themselves—they want their "us" moment. They've continuously slammed and slandered BLM, pushing their agendas by twisting the message into a completely different meaning that says *only* Black lives matter or that Black lives matter *more*. They say "all lives matter"—and of course all lives matter—but *all* lives aren't in danger. They don't want us to notice the injustice. They don't want us to have an opinion. They want us to sit our Black asses down and shut up. That's not going to happen. We will never convenience them by being as ignorant as they want us to be.

We have to stop politicizing the BLM movement. Conservatives often narrate it as a far-left extremist group to justify their opposition to it, but this movement is not a Liberal issue. Black Lives Matter is a social justice issue, and a social justice issue is a *human* issue. Black Lives Matter is a movement to dismantle racism. Bigots want you to believe that if you think Black lives matter, you're "anti-police," which is "anti-American." The Conservative agenda has been to paint BLM as a Marxist movement whose objective is complete anarchy. To counter this, they've staged anti-BLM protests where they wave their Trump flags for his glory. This flag, much like his MAGA cap, has become yet another symbol of White supremacy.

BLM protests led to the deconstructing of many Confederate monuments. These Confederate monuments were meant to intimidate Black people and to isolate them from society after the Civil War—a war in which soldiers were ultimately fighting to defend slavery. BLM protests also, unfortunately, led to many riots across the country. Whether out of sheer anger and frustration regarding constant injustices or out of selfish apathy, many people resorted to violence and looting. It was saddening to see the chaos distract from the message behind the peaceful protests. It was also upsetting to see those who were against the movement showing up just to add fuel to the fires—like a certain teen from Illinois who deliberately drove into the fray in Wisconsin looking for an opportunity to shoot someone, yet Trump and his Conservatives consider him a hero for "defending his country."

It almost seems like the 2020 BLM movement coinciding with the pandemic was necessary because it forced everyone to stop and pay attention to what's going on. The coronavirus seems to mirror the virus of racism. The frustration of a global lockdown because of Covid caused the perfect storm for chaos. In the midst of this storm, however, many eyes were finally opened. People and corporations around the world suddenly realized that they need to speak up and stand in solidarity with the cause. They realized that if racial injustice affects some of us, it really does affect us all. It's beautiful to see true *diversity* come together to stand up for Black lives.

Unfortunately, There are allies and supporters of BLM who don't even know what it's about. Many of them joined the protests just to get out of the house during the Covid lockdown. NFL Commissioner Roger Goodell decided four years later that Black lives matter when not saying so became a financial risk. Meanwhile, Kaepernick has yet to be offered an invitation to return to the league. I just wish more people genuinely cared about the movement, and not just because it affects their bottom line. We would see better change if more people cared about the injustices of Black people, even if it doesn't affect them directly.

An age of reckoning is upon us. We have begun a new civil rights movement to right civil wrongs. We will continue to protest and call out every injustice until everyone knows—whether they want to or not—that Black lives matter.

## *Transracial: The Inappropriateness of Cultural Appropriation*

Why is it that White privilege is exclusive, but Black culture is communal? Thanks to social media, Black culture belongs to everybody. More and more White people are appropriating Black culture, and many pander to us presumably out of "White guilt." Some White people even attempt to pass as a Black person. They dress themselves in a figurative—or sometimes literal—Blackface and proceed to offend. Every Halloween, you'll see White people wearing Black people as costumes while their more bigoted counterparts decorate their trees with lynched niggers in effigy.

For ages, White people—especially bodybuilders—have tanned themselves to an almost minstrel-like version of us. Today, this has morphed into Blackfishing in which White—or non-Black—people darken their skin and assume Black traits in order to pass as Black. For social media influencers, Blackfishing has become a form of cosplay with which mainly White women assume an ethnic ambiguity to utilize racial opportunism. These self-entitled White influencers play a dress-up game of "let me borrow your culture" on a daily basis for praise and for profit. They're seen by sponsors as exotic and versatile, effectively stealing opportunities from people who actually represent the culture from which they "borrow." This behavior follows a centuries-long history of White people buying and selling our culture.

These culture vultures steal from our style and unique customs, and they're praised for it. They're seen as edgy and innovative, whereas we're seen as "ghetto" and uncivilized for embodying the very things that they steal from us. When someone like Miley Cyrus shakes her ass on the VMA stage, the mainstream of White America thinks that she invented twerking. When a Kardashian injects her lips or her ass to look fuller, these features are suddenly in style. They wonder why we get offended by this, but what are we supposed to think when the world says that Black features and fashion aren't beautiful unless they're on someone who isn't Black? Society seems to love Black culture, but they don't have that same love for Black people.

People don't seem to understand that cultural appropriation isn't the same thing as cultural appreciation. Many White people steal music, fashion, and ideas from Black culture under the guise of being "inspired," while some claim that we're all the same in order to deny us due credit. They profit from everything that we do and everything that we are, and White executives in every arena make billions of dollars off of us without ever truly investing in us. How is it that we don't seem to benefit—in any way—from the commodification of our culture?

Today, we have apps like Urban Dictionary to help keep White people in touch with Black culture. These apps are almost exclusively ran by groups of White male yuppies and hipsters who find it extremely necessary to define our vernacular for us and to decode it for themselves. I don't understand why some White people feel the need to speak the slang that we speak in an effort to relate to us. After all, we're still people, fully capable of speaking and understanding fluent English. They've even added words and phrases like "throwing shade" to the Oxford dictionary—after over three decades of Black people using these terms—just because enough White people decided to adopt the affectation.

White people can conveniently remove the Black affectation like an article of clothing when it starts to become too much of a hindrance. They can walk the walk and talk the talk, but they don't have to deal with any of the consequences of being Black. They trivialize our culture—reducing it to a disposable fashion—and the worst part of it all is that they don't seem to get how insulting it is. It often feels as if they're mocking us, transferring themselves so casually and carelessly into our Black, unprivileged world.

The leaders of this Blackfishing, appropriation movement seem to be the daughters of Kris Jenner. Their influence has made it acceptable for the White female to masquerade as an off-White "other." In addition to appropriating virtually every aspect of Black culture, the Kardashian clan use Black men as disposable accessories. This Caucasian Armenian family has birthed a rapidly-expanding generation of mixed Black children, as if to give license to their appropriation. Their ignorant cultural mindset is inevitably passed on to their enormous social media following who—quite literally—don't know any better.

White people often appropriate different cultures to make themselves seem more interesting. It's like being White makes them a blank canvas to paint with whichever ethnic colors they choose. The fact that they feel like they can pick and choose their culture—and even their ethnicity—is the epitome of White privilege. You can't be culturally fluid, much less adopt another culture as your personality. I read a comment from a White man who—growing up in the '80s—was taught that America was a melting pot, and he took that to mean that White people should meld with other cultures. Because he felt like he didn't have a culture of his own due to being White, he was confused, and he began to fetishize other cultures.

In one of the more extreme cases of Blackfishing, a White woman named Rachel Dolezal infamously transitioned her race to become—at least in her mind—a Black woman. She even changed her name to the "African-sounding" Nkechi Amare Diallo. The delusionally "transracial" Dolezal wanted to victimize herself with Blackness. Somehow, she seemed to equate being Black with suffering, and she was all too eager to take on the role of martyr. The audacity of a White woman defiantly appropriating the Black race is evidence of her not understanding her White privilege.

It's crazy how many White people think that they get a "Black pass" just because they're in a relationship with a Black person. They think that this gives them license to use the n-word, make stereotypical remarks, and basically appropriate every aspect of Black culture. We're well aware that there are White people who befriend, marry, and/or have children with Black people just for some imaginary "Black by association" card. This gives them the false impression that it's impossible for them to be racist while simultaneously giving them false permission to be racist. It's ridiculous how people can feel like they're an exception to racism and oppression by way of some arbitrary technicality.

Black people are often too eager to invite White people to "the cookout." Moreover, instead of wanting them to appreciate us, we want them to act like us. We then get upset when they appropriate, steal from, and take credit for our culture. For this, we have to take responsibility. We often get too comfortable with White people and confuse them by calling them "my nigga," which makes them get too comfortable with us. They see this as us giving them approval to use this term at their disposal. There always seems to be an exception made for context, but context is irrelevant in regards to this word. The word *nigger/nigga* is going to mean the same thing no matter how you twist it to justify using it, and if you have to justify using any word, that should tell you that you're not supposed to be using it in the first place.

It's hard for me to understand the White person's obsession with "nigga." To me, it seems to be their vital necessity in assimilating Black culture—to complete the "look." Ironically, it's White privilege that gives them the expectation of being entitled to use this word. There was a time when White guys who "acted Black" were called "wiggers," and many of them wore it as a badge of honor. That same wigger mentality makes White people—who are desperate to be a part of the culture—blind to any "nigga" restrictions. As White people, there's simply no way you can say that you have love and respect for Black people and still use this word. Also, as Black people, we have to stop enabling this behavior.

If you're a White person, it doesn't matter if you were adopted by a Black family or if every person you know is Black; you will never know what it's like to be Black. It doesn't make sense for you to feel like you can identify with our plight because the world doesn't see you—or treat you—as a Black person. Cultural appropriation is a disrespectful spit in the face. It's important for all people to know that Black is not a personality, Black is not a social class, and Black is not a sum of personal worth.

**FABIAN M.C. KUYKENDALL**

## Negro Nazi: The Self-Oppression of Black People

For the younger generation of Black people, we need to redefine what it means to be Black. Too many people believe that being Black means being "real," which means being "hood" or "ratchet." That basically makes us mediocre beings who can only aspire to a marginal level of intelligence. Why would we limit ourselves that way? Why are we so proud to have this ratchet righteousness? Of course, there are many Black people who are raised in housing projects and other drug, gang, and crime-infested environments, but why are we so determined to believe that these things should define us?

We need to stop equating ratchetness with being "real." Too many Black men insist that they're the "realest nigga" as if it's an accurate statement or even a good thing to be. They attach to it a definition of a man who takes pride in revolving his life around the streets, selling drugs instead of working honestly, being incarcerated, being violent, and basically doing anything to earn that pathetic "credibility." A real nigga isn't a nigga at all, he's an upstanding, self-assured, respectable Black man. He's a man who's secure enough to go against the degrading stereotypes that too many of us continue to live up to. Realness is having the courage to be better than what the bigots of society want you to be. Realness is being fearless enough to be exactly who you are without feeling the need to prove your realness to the streets or to justify your worth to the world.

We often judge each other based on the way that we talk and act, insisting that speaking in an educated, grammatically correct manner equates to "talking White." Somehow, our ignorance convinces us that intelligence is reserved exclusively for White people. Too many of us resist education and mock those of us who pursue it. We're lost in the perdition of mental and environmental impoverishment, and—because misery loves company—we hold each other back. Why do we do this to each other? It's like being stranded on an island of desolation and setting fire to the one lifeboat that washes ashore.

Black culture has many customs, traditions, and styles that are beautiful, so why do we always highlight the uncultured, unsophisticated, uncivilized aspects of our people? We'd rather call ourselves real niggas and bad bitches instead of brothers and sisters or kings and queens. Essentially, this reinforces many White people's negative perception of us, which gives them an excuse to treat us accordingly. We have to stop allowing White people to exploit us. I'm tired of seeing Black people on low-class reality shows produced by White people who profit from our ignorant ratchetness. We also have to stop supporting our own exploitation by watching such buffoonery.

We have a history of giving our children "Black names" like Shaniqua and LeMarcus without realizing the societal stigma attached to these names. Most people automatically assume that people with "Black names" are uneducated and uncivilized. There's also a blatant corporate bias against these names. Studies have shown that people with "Black names" are more likely to have their resume overlooked and denied an opportunity to interview for a position simply because of their name. This is an unfortunate reality that we have to think about. It doesn't mean that we should allow ourselves to be controlled by the stereotypes that *they* place on us, but we have to find a balance. There's a blurry line between Black pride and ratchet ignorance.

It's been said that if Dr. Martin Luther King Jr. were alive today, he wouldn't be surprised by White people calling us "niggers;" he'd be surprised that we use that word to refer to each other. At the 2016 White House Correspondents Dinner, comedian Larry Wilmore referred to the first Black President of the United States—Barack Obama—as "my nigga." Is there ever a place and time when we can just be people? It's shameful that we see ourselves as niggas. When will we realize that we are so much better than that word? We claim that we take away its power through the context in which we use it and that it holds no power over us. However, if it's almost impossible for us not to use this word in daily conversation, then it actually does have power over us.

Former presidential candidate, Dr. Ben Carson made a statement to CNN that President Obama was "raised White" due to his middle-class upbringing. Because Obama "went to private schools" and "grew up in a relatively affluent environment," apparently this makes him less of a Black person. It saddens me to see Black people being generalized and marginalized by other Black people. How dare we expect more for ourselves if we don't believe that these things were meant for us to have? Dr. Carson has also referred to slaves as "immigrants." The fact that he, a well-educated Black man, would affect that type of blindness—presumably in the name of White acceptance—just speaks to his diluted character.

In a way that seems to be more prevalent than in other cultures, Black people don't support each other enough. We tend to have jealousy and hatred toward one another based on looks, wealth, and success. When one of us has an achievement that breaks new ground, we find ways to invalidate it, thereby standing in the way of our own progression. We call each other a "sellout" simply for succeeding. I believe that most of us harbor a self-hate, of which we're still unaware. Anytime we see an instance of Black excellence, a lot of us have a knee-jerk reaction of negativity because we've been brainwashed into thinking that we don't deserve it. It's sad that we see each other in the same way as the bigots do.

Black self-hate also manifests itself in the form of colorism or prejudice against other Black people with darker skin tones. This leads some victims of colorism to extreme behavior like bleaching their skin. These victims experience the trauma of an upbringing that includes other Black kids calling them names like "tar baby" and being made to feel like less of a person, even by their own families. As Black people, we all were raised in families of varying skin tones and have seen lighter relatives be treated far more favorably than darker ones.

Over generations, we've been indoctrinated by society to believe that lighter is better. Having a deep, dark skin tone doesn't equate to beauty by the world's standards. Shamefully, we pass down White people's prejudice of us to each other and compete for social position based on who has the lighter skin tone. This stems from the division of the "house nigger" and the "field nigger" in the days of slavery and has led to the self-stratification of the "brown paper bag test." Since then, there has always been a perception of privilege for light-skinned, mixed-race Black people. Today, Black people and Black customs aren't generally accepted unless they've been diluted with White.

For many decades, there has been a—for the most part—friendly competition among Black men in regards to skin tone (dark skin vs. light skin). We've gone back and forth about whose complexion was "in style" at the moment. Although we tease each other all in good fun, there's also colorism against lighter-skinned Black men. These men get labeled as being "soft," "weak," "pretty boys," or simply less than Black. We need to stop acting like a person's Blackness isn't Black enough just because they have a lighter complexion or because they're mixed with another race, it's just ignorant.

There was a time—probably dating back to the '80s or '90s—when interracial relationships between Black people and White people were taboo. Today, many Black men seem to idealize the White woman. They see the White woman as a status symbol, a trophy, an exclusive high-end brand. These Black men and White women frequently show each other off on social media like fashion trends as their relationships are perceived to be mutual exchanges of a cultural "come-up." On the other end, some White men seem to fetishize the Black woman—which isn't a compliment because when you fetishize someone, you're devaluing them as a person. From the outside, the relationship often looks like that of a slave master and his bed wench. Some Black people can't seem to break free from the mental bondage of perceived White perfection.

As Black men, we too often mistreat and fail to support and protect Black women. For generations, we've failed to set a positive example. It saddens me to see Black men and women fighting with each other on social media like Republicans and Democrats. Many Black men will defend White women like police officers while all too eagerly attacking Black women with venomous self-hate. When did selling out become a good look for Black men? We barely even showed up to protest our injustices in 2020 while our female counterparts—and White allies—marched religiously in our defense. We owe Black women so much more than what we give them. They're our mothers, daughters, sisters, aunties, cousins, and grandmothers. We must love, respect, support, and protect them at all costs.

There are people outside of our melanated circle who covertly create these digital wildfires on social media that encourage us to destroy each other, and we keep taking the bait. They just sit back with their popcorn watching and laughing at our gullible ignorance. Why is it so easy for us to make each other the enemy? Why is it so hard for us to see that our division is only conquering us? We didn't create this war that we're fighting, so what are we even fighting for? We don't have to agree with each other, but everyone is so desperate to be right. It seems like we're in competition to show the rest of the world that we're the "good Black" by separating ourselves from each other. However, there is no hierarchical system of Blackness.

Many Black Conservatives seem to confuse condemning and selling out their race with being freethinking and revolutionary. I believe that's why they're so quick to jump on the bandwagon of someone like Donald Trump. When these people reach a certain level of wealth and privilege, they seem to believe that "Black people problems" don't apply to them. Political shock talker Candace Owens—much like former Fox News contributor Stacey Dash—is a Black woman who, by mere observation, appears to be anti-Black. She seems to think that the more she hates Black people, the more White people will accept her. People like her seem to have a "Black guilt"—or racial Stockholm syndrome—which makes them sympathize with their racist oppressors. They minimize themselves and their race in an effort to appease White people and to basically say "sorry for being Black."

It seems to me that Kanye West basically wants to be the Black Trump, and he would do and say whatever it takes to make that his reality. What's disturbing—and potentially dangerous—is someone like West supporting Trump mainly to go against the norm and be "different." Because he's an independent thinker lost in an exclusive world of concession, he doesn't seem to understand the implications and consequences of such baseless actions. This is the negligent energy that led him to make reprehensible remarks like "Slavery was a choice."

West had no reservations about kissing Trump's ass, denouncing Jewish people, praising Hitler, and completely selling out the Black community. His coonish behavior also includes wearing a "White Lives Matter" shirt—along with his fellow Sunken Place cell mate Candace Owens—to antagonize Black people. His delusion has become painfully obvious, which makes it nearly impossible to take him seriously. He's so desperate to prove that his way of thinking is revolutionary that he seems to believe that his reckless actions are justified. It's just a shame that these reckless actions come at the expense of his own people.

I feel like many Black people think that they can't be successful unless they adopt conservative values—like they have to be obsequiously indebted to the White man to achieve anything worthwhile. I think that this makes it easy for them to just accept racism or pretend that it doesn't exist. For them, adopting conservative values means "ascending" to a higher level of Blackness where acknowledging racial injustice somehow means playing the victim. Once they're accepted into the great White world, they don't seem to have any qualms about abandoning they're race. While I do believe in a lot of the ideology of Black Conservatives, I don't understand why this ideology has to be under the umbrella of Conservatism. Why can't this be an independent mindset and not tied to a political organization that almost exclusively benefits White people?

Truth be told, Black people depend on White people far too much. Too many of us believe that we can't have anything unless they give it to us, and too many of them believe the same. We give them too much power to dictate how our lives should be run and too much credit for what we have. For that reason, our reliance on government assistance has to stop. We have to pay attention and realize how much it impairs us by giving us an excuse to be lazy and not have to work to earn a better living. We also need to wake up and see that this "assistance" isn't actually intended to help us at all. It's meant to keep us in the same lower-class state of mind and existence so that we won't strive for more in the name of education, career advancement, or any other opportunities for growth and success.

It is imperative that we stick together, support each other, and not allow ourselves to be divided and conquered. Just like family, we won't agree on everything, but we can't let our disagreements cause us to turn our backs on each other. Everyone has an opinion, so you can't expect everyone to share the same passion or outrage over every single thing that you feel is important. Let's stop judging and casting each other out over differences of opinion. We have to remember that we're in this together, fighting the exact same fight. If racism and injustice affects one of us, it truly affects us all.

We can preach that Black lives matter, but we have to start living like we matter. Can you imagine where we'd be if Black lives mattered to more Black people?

We have to stop helping the bigots kill us. We also have to stop protecting each other's ignorant actions out of fear of being a "snitch." With all of the Black on Black violence we see on a daily basis, we've developed a sort of urban post-traumatic stress disorder. Not only do we have to worry about racist White people and racist White cops, we also have to worry about other Black people and self-hating Black cops—like the ones who beat and murdered Tyre Nichols. Sadly, we keep passing a culture of violence to every new generation.

In Black households, it's very common to do so, but we have to stop beating our children. You can call it "spanking" or "disciplining," but it's still a beating and it only perpetuates the cycle of slavery. Slave masters would beat their slaves for pretty much the same reason we beat our children, misbehavior and disobedience. This was to keep the slave's submission in tact so that the slave master could retain his power. We must stop treating our children as slaves and learn how to parent and discipline them. If you can't discipline your child without beating them—or if he or she won't listen to you otherwise—it's because they don't respect you as a parent. Beating your child is just a lazy alternative to being a real parent and doing the work of properly raising your child. End the cycle.

Some of our formally enslaved ancestors actually owned slaves themselves. They learned from their oppressors how to oppress their own. Today, we continue to pass down this slave master mentality without even knowing. We are an oppressed people begotten by generations of oppressed people. Why would we want to add to that oppression by oppressing ourselves?

## *Fault & Default: Eugenics & The Racial Whitening of America*

As the racial majority in America, it seems that White people are the default race. Black people—along with other racial minorities—are made to be the faulty race. White people constructed this hierarchical power structure to label us as minorities whom they see as minor. Because they come from a long lineage of White supremacy, I believe that White people are inherently racist; that's why—most of the time—they don't even realize their racist actions. Too many of them don't see racism for what it is; they see it, instead, as their birthright.

Eugenics was and is yet another justification of hate and is basically scientific racism. It attempts to create "perfect" human beings whom—of course—are White. Eugenicists aim to improve the genetic quality of the human population by eliminating those "unfit to reproduce." These bigoted "scientists" make it clear that there's a significant difference in class among races: There's Black and there's right.

The Nordic race is viewed by Nordicists—or White supremacists—as a superior racial group. The Aryan "master race" of Nazi ideology is said to be the pinnacle of racial hierarchy simply based on phenotypical traits. When someone is said to have "all-American good looks," he or she is usually tall and athletic with blonde hair and blue eyes. Of course, a majority race would consider themselves superior to the point of self-indulgent narcissism. This Nordicism promotes a racist, White-ist delusion of grandeur across the whole White world.

Nordicists are strictly anti-miscegenation as they don't want "mud races" tainting their pure Whiteness. While in office, Donald Trump—regarding immigration—referred to non-White countries like Haiti, El Salvador, and some parts of Africa as "shithole countries." He stated that he would rather have immigrants from countries like lily-White Norway because—in my opinion—he believes that White is the superior race. Trump remains a hero to alt-right hate groups who—because of his leadership—feel like their White supremacist views and actions are justified.

America is clearly afraid of the dark. There's such a stigma on the word *black* that Black people are seen as a black plague, and, in America, black plague equals Black death. Racial Whitening means eliminating Black people and preventing their advancement by any means necessary. Scientific racists have used forced or clandestine sterilization to control the Black population. They've also used Black people as lab rats to conduct their evil trials—like the infamous Tuskegee experiment. Black slaves were seen as only 3/5 of a person. There was even a time when Black people were put on display in human zoos.

The racial Whitening of America is much like the colonization of Alkebu-lan by Europeans who gave it the slave name, Africa. There's a theory that Hispanics in America are urged to identify as White when filling out federal documents. By doing so, this makes the White census appear to be greater than it actually is. People have managed to White-wash even the most trivial things; that's why there's white gold, white chocolate, white bread, white rice, white-collar crimes, even white lies. White people continue to White-wash history, laws, policies, and boardrooms to maintain a systemic advantage over minorities and to ingrain White supremacy into the consciousness of Americans.

Too many people fall for the idea of White perfection. To some degree, we've all been brainwashed by the perceived European ideal when it comes to looks, fashion, art, and education. This is the reason many people of color reproduce with people of White. This is the reason many people of color bleach their skin. This is the reason White people "validate" Black culture. This is the reason racism persists.

Racism is a defect, be it genetic or environmental. It's a mental illness—a psychosis that makes psychotic people. Racism is irrational, and because it's irrational, racist people will never have a good enough reason for it. Eugenics was, is, and will always be an ignorant pacification of the White supremacist's insecurity. There is no supreme race.

## *Unapologetic Blackness: Being Comfortable in Black Skin*

Sometimes, I feel like I have to talk to White people in a way that doesn't frighten or offend them—like I have to be timid, even apologetic in my approach. This is because I know that when they see me—6 feet, 3 inches, and 217 pounds of male Blackness—they see an intimidating object of mystery that is to be feared. In their midst, I can't help but feel like my mere presence is offensive. It's a shame that my skin tone isn't conducive to me going about my day in a comfortable manner. I'm conspicuously Black.

It's been ingrained into my subconscious that I should forgo my own feelings and go out of my way to make White people feel comfortable with me, what a weird burden. When I drive through a White neighborhood or pull up to a store parking lot, I instinctively turn down the music in my car. I'm overly conscious of the way that I dress and the way that I talk. I feel like I have to have an exaggerated affability to offset their preconceived negative expectation of people like me. I'm unmistakably Black.

It's evident that we live in a nation that only accepts a diluted Blackness—a nation where we have to be tentatively, cautiously, and passively Black. Our Blackness has to be infused with a White sensibility to be palatable to their majority. It's almost like we're required to be ashamed of our Blackness and expected to suppress it just to meet their approval. For some reason, we carry this notion that we have to be on our absolute best behavior in front of White people. It's like they are the authority, and we have to tread lightly in *their* space.

Somehow, we feel like we have an obligation to be a representation for all Black people. It bothers me when Black people tolerate—or even condone—racism in order to appease White people. We seem to be so preoccupied with trying to prove to White people that we are the exception to their stereotypes, but the truth is, any stereotype they have of Black people will exist whether they see you or not. What we need to ask ourselves is: Why is it our obligation to make racists less racist?—to remind them that Black lives matter?—to forgive their racism?

There have been studies that show the effects of being Black within the racial tension of America. Some people have compared the daily microaggressions experienced by Black people to post-traumatic stress. These experiences are said to have infected us with a general degree of anxiety and depression. I know firsthand how hard it is to be Black and the stigma attached to it. It's been said that the most dangerous place for a Black person to live is in the mind of someone who isn't Black. Because we're extremely aware of this, we're constantly on the lookout for racial drive-bys, almost to the point of paranoia. I often find myself in a state of silent defensiveness, like I have to sully my own mood out of expectation of their racism until they prove otherwise. Anytime I'm treated unfairly by someone of another race, I can't help but wonder if it's because of mine.

Some White people claim that Black people always play the race card, but it's those same people who constantly remind us that we're Black. They even manage to play the role of the oppressor and the victim simultaneously. With some White people calling us out for "reverse racism," I've had to ask myself, "Can Black people really be racist?" I've come to realize that, while Black people can certainly be *prejudiced* against other races, it's impossible for us to be *racist* by true definition of the word. For example—as a minority—we don't have the power to enforce biased actions against an entire race, whereas White people can utilize their majority to create laws that basically make it even harder to be Black. That's racist.

Mongers of hate are desperate to be acknowledged, but we have to stop buying into their plans. More importantly, we have to stop spreading their message; this includes reposting all of the racist memes, texts, and images that come across the web every day. It only glorifies the hate by saturating social media and polluting social conscious with such ignorance. We don't need to constantly see and hear about these racist instances to know that racism and bigoted mindsets exist. What we should post on social media are images that are completely antithetical to the negativity that we're used to seeing. Let's counter the hate with images of our beautiful people of color graduating from medical school, performing at Carnegie Hall, or receiving a medal of honor for their military service.

I believe that protests—especially rallies—against racial injustices are mostly ineffective. Many people only protest to be a part of the chaos. America is a massive corporation disguised as a nation, and it's premier motivation is equity, not equality. Therefore, it only makes sense to boycott these White-owned big businesses—Walmart, Apple, Amazon, etc.—out of protest. There are so many Black-owned businesses in America which we—as Black people—have the power to turn into billion-dollar corporations and claim more power for ourselves. The problem is, most of us have been programmed to believe that White-owned corporations are somehow better, and we fear missing out on the same privileges as the majority.

An unfortunate reality with most Black people is that we don't know our history or our heritage, all we seem to know is that our ancestors were slaves. Our history was stolen from us the same way we were stolen from our land. All of our customs, our language, our style, and our essence was erased by the White man and replaced with a lifeless subservience. What once was a rich culture—which would have been passed down for generations—is lost on us today. It is our duty to recapture this essence and to learn who we really are.

We are descendants of African royalty. Mansa Musa—ruler of the 14th century Mali Empire and often referred to as the richest person in history—is an opulent example of Black wealth. We should realize our own Black excellence and take pride in the magic of our melanin. We should celebrate our culture—as well as our ancestors—by letting our freedom flags fly for every Juneteenth. We should own the uniqueness of who we are and acknowledge the beauty in the variety of hues, shapes, styles, lifestyles, and personalities we compile. Black people are not monolithic. Africa is a continent, not a country.

Even if we are the victim, let's not be victimized. We give racists too much credit by allowing them to hold us back. We have to stop applying convenient double standards to White people that encourage them to cry "reverse racism." We have to remove the race card from the deck, no exceptions, no excuses. We don't need to justify our race, all we need to do is continue being Black.

In spite of what's acceptable, I am shamelessly, relentlessly, unapologetically Black. No longer will I apologize for taking up too much space. I'm Black and I'm not sorry.

## *All-American: Diversity vs. Division*

What is all-American? When I hear this term, I picture 1950s suburban America with picket fences as white as their owners. *All-American* is most commonly used to represent athletes, but it also represents the American ideal. What does an American look like? To the average American, an American looks like a blue-collar Midwesterner and his or her family. They live in the country and listen to country music in their pickup truck, which they park in the garage of their middle-class home. In other words, the average American is White.

Truth be told, America belongs to Native Americans. This country was stolen from them as it was pillaged by Europeans. Now, the European influence of White supremacy is what has come to define America. We've broiled way past the melting point of this so-called melting pot. The majority of people have no idea what (ethnic) diversity is. More often than not, they seem to associate it with the inclusion of Black people. However, diversity demands variety. Diversity is Black people, White people, Native Americans, Hispanics, Asians, Pacific Islanders, etc. all sharing the land of the United States.

In the world of color and contrast, white is the presence of light, and black is the absence of light, making them polar opposites. In the world of race and diversity, however, what we need to realize is that Black is not the opposite of White. The two should not be compared as good vs. evil, pretty vs. ugly, or even Black vs. White. Believe it or not, this is not a Black and White world. Somehow—in our selfish war of races—we've managed to forget that we share this planet with a spectrum of beautiful ethnic colors.

In 1997, there was a television broadcasting of an updated version of the beloved story of *Cinderella*, which had a multi-racial cast. The role of Cinderella was portrayed by a Black woman—Brandy Norwood—who marries an Asian prince, who has a White father, who has a Black wife, etc. Even though the broadcast was beautifully produced, garnered over 60 million viewers, and went on to receive multiple awards and nominations, the main focus of critics was the color(s) of the cast. To many of these critics, it was unacceptable to have a multi-racial cast because it broke away from "tradition." The problem with the United States is that its tradition is somehow only seen as White despite the other races in occupancy.

Uneducated racists are quick to say, "If you don't like it here, go back to Africa." How can we go back to somewhere we've never been? Idiot. In that case, *you* brought us over here, so why don't *you* take us back against our will and see how that works out for you. These same racists also have a deep hatred for immigrants whom they feel should "speak English" or "speak American." Many White people—as the majority and default race—seem to think that all other races should adjust to their customs. They defend this way of thinking by saying, "This is America," implying that this is *their* country, but forgetting the unifying principle of what America is supposed to represent.

In an effort to appease the "true Americans," immigrants often feel the need to assimilate to our culture by replacing their names with Americanized alternatives. They're often told that their names are too much trouble to spell or pronounce. They make every effort to hide their ethnic origin out of fear of being alienated or ostracized in America. What many of us fail to remember is that—other than Native Americans—we're all immigrants to some degree. This is the *United* States of America, where people of all ethnicities, colors, and cultures come to unite. No one who enters America should have to undergo some forced assimilation.

Many immigrants learn about Black people by watching the news. Unfortunately, what they often see are images of Black people being killed, attacked, arrested, and narrated as menacing beasts to be hated and feared. Every ethnic culture in the world has been conditioned to hate Black people. They see us as unattractive, uncivilized, and dangerous. This is exactly why representation matters. Every race and ethnicity needs to see positive representations of themselves in news and media, and we all should promote positive representations of ourselves to ensure that other cultures get the full picture of who we really are.

The song "Lift Every Voice and Sing" is often referred to as the Black national anthem. EGOT-winning actress and co-host of *The View* Whoopi Goldberg argued that this anthem should be sung in conjunction with the national anthem at sporting events. I disagree. While it goes without saying that America has dealt countless inequities to Black people, the national anthem represents *America*, for better or worse. We can't expect this country to acknowledge a separate anthem for every race or ethnic group because it goes against what is supposed to be one nation. "Lift Every Voice and Sing" is an anthem for *us* as Black people, and we shouldn't feel like we need recognition from the rest of the country to validate it.

Why is it such a big deal that a woman, a gay person, or a Black person is just as capable of having a major accomplishment as any White person? Why are we still surprised when this happens? As a Black person, it's always a proud, inspiring moment when someone becomes the first Black President of the United States, the first Black billionaire, the first Black Pulitzer Prize winner, etc. However—in this day and age—why is it necessary to constantly preface these unprecedented achievements with "the first Black …?" Today, any mention of "the first" is almost exclusively used in reference to Black people and other minorities, not White people.

To me, such a statement just says that we as minorities aren't expected to achieve the same levels of success as White people. Furthermore, I believe it diminishes that success by implying that it was only impressive by the low minority standard—"That was pretty good … for a Black person." Also, Black people shouldn't feel like they have to wait for another Black person to achieve greatness in order to believe that it's possible. Sure, most people love being the first to reach certain milestones, but success shouldn't have a color. I look forward to the day when there are no more "first Black …," "first female …," or "first gay …" milestones left to occur.

Most corporations implement a workplace culture of PC diversity. This sentiment somehow comes off as forced and disingenuous. You have to wonder, if businesses weren't required to hire those token ethnics, disabled veterans, or open homosexuals, how often would they? It's a shame that Affirmative Action is still needed today and that companies have to mention that they're an Equal Opportunity Employer in order for some minority groups to feel secure enough to apply for employment. It's also a shame that there have to be protected classes for people in order to prevent employment discrimination.

We often hear about racism, sexism, and heterosexism, but we don't talk enough about ageism. Once people reach middle age, they're regularly overlooked and dismissed by society. It's amazing how much we judge each other based on age—how we look at someone differently once we learn how old they are. It's foolish how we let age determine a person's capability and value. We also frequently neglect to acknowledge ableism. We look at people with physical and mental limitations as less than human. We're recklessly insensitive with our language, using words like *retarded, lame, blind, deaf,* and *psycho.* At the very least, we need to learn to be more respectful to our diverse population in the name of inclusivity.

When it comes to gender and civil rights—often times—there are White women who cry for an equality that doesn't seem to include Black people. Meanwhile, they don't have a problem using Black people to help gain a victory for themselves. First of all, there is no equality unless *all* people are equal. There's no such thing as "separate but equal," it just doesn't work. I believe that all minority groups should support each other as allies. We shouldn't treat each other like disposable aid.

I never realized that Band-Aids were made to be flesh-colored. Their original color is obviously one that's tailored to the skin tone of a White person. It wasn't until 2020 that Band-Aid finally started to produce their product in various shades of brown to represent the wide spectrum of races and skin tones in the world. Nevertheless, it's good to see the idea of diversity spreading to where you'd probably least expect it.

Why isn't there a Latin race? It's weird how they have to identify racially as White or Black, but they're still seen in society as Latin or Hispanic. Most Latin people themselves say that they don't fit in the boxes that the American Census tries to force them into. Having them basically choose their race seems to benefit the numbers of the White majority. In the meantime, Latin people are essentially robbed of their own unique racial identity. The same can be said for people of Middle Eastern and North African ethnicity. Why isn't there a

MENA race? They clearly don't fit into a Black or White box, yet the senseless Census of our White American government says that they're White.

The distinction of race vs. ethnicity will always be debated, especially since race is socially constructed. It only becomes more muddled when races are mixed. Why are biracial people—specifically Black and White—obligated to identify only as Black? Why must they choose one race and deny the other, in essence denying their father or mother? It's been said that if you have one drop of Black ancestry, it effectively taints the rest of your racial makeup, therefore making you Black. Mixed race people are often left with a sense of racial ambiguity, which makes them feel like they don't belong. We used to distinguish them simply as "other." This so-called one-drop rule is bullshit.

What if race and gender were as interchangeable as clothing where everyone could essentially be a different person every day? Would you change who you are just to join the majority? What if race and ethnicity were random at birth where one who is Black could birth one who is Asian, or one who is Hispanic could birth one who is White? Would you be happy with your child if they weren't the color you wanted them to be? Would racism still exist? It's been theorized that one day, all races will merge into one; perhaps that's the only way that race won't matter.

I read an article about a college fraternity that wanted to remain all-White. Initially, I saw this as a racist club of White elitists, but after further thought, I realized that there are also all-Black fraternities, Asian clubs, Latin clubs, etc. Minority fraternities or clubs tend to form as a result of discrimination from White people, which is why I felt a little uneasy about this all-White fraternity. However, they have the same right to stick with their race and culture as we all do. Furthermore, if any all-White fraternity had racist intentions, I would want nothing to do with it anyway.

We should all remember that just because America is diverse doesn't mean that it should be divided. I believe that all races or ethnic groups should be allowed to take pride in their culture without being made to feel prejudiced. I also believe that our cultural differences make us special, so we should be able to come together to share those differences and learn from one another.

It's been written that my hometown of Milwaukee, WI is one of America's most segregated cities, making it a microcosm of the country itself. It's sad that with all of the diversity in America, we still remain segregated, afraid to homogenize. We're not living up to the name of our country. The United States of America can't be united when there's no unity. America should be an amalgamation of different cultures. It's those differences that make us all the same. We all share this country. We're all-American. We're *all* American.

# CHAPTER 3 - POLITICS & GOVERNMENT

<hr>

### *What Goes Up Goes Corrupt: The American Government*

The American government has a centuries-long history of being a nefariously covert organization. From presidents to senators to federal judges, the system is filled with corruption. What they hide from us in the darkness and what eventually comes to light are reasons why we can't trust our government.

It's become evident with our government that a position of power soon becomes an abuse of power. The Internal Revenue Service (IRS) uses taxes as an excuse for financial rape, callously feeding federal cupidity. There have been cases of the Federal Bureau of Investigation (FBI) bribing judges for information and suspension of evidence. The Central Intelligence Agency (CIA) has had an extensive involvement in illegal activity including domestic spying, drug trafficking—It's been said that the CIA played a major role in the crack epidemic of the '80s—and, of course, Watergate.

The Watergate scandal is probably the most infamous abuse of power the American presidency has ever seen. President Nixon's gang of corrupt government officials burglarized the DNC headquarters at the Watergate Complex and wiretapped their phones. Nixon and his administration made a cover-up effort, which included destroying evidence. He also had the CIA block an FBI investigation of the crimes. The burglars were paid hush money, and Nixon had his aides lie about his knowledge of the burglary. Nixon resigned to dodge impeachment and—for his troubles—was granted a full pardon by his successor, President Ford. Unbelievable.

The CIA is known for its clandestine—and often illegal—operations. One of its infamous mind control experiments known as MK-Ultra involved psychological torture including electroshock, paralytics, and high doses of LSD. The unwitting subjects of these experiments endured permanent psychological and physical damage, many died. They were treated like human lab rats for the sake of developing methods of mind control, which the CIA ultimately realized wasn't possible. The CIA destroyed (almost) all records of MK-Ultra, so we can only imagine the extent of the evils they carried out. The CIA has decades of secrets and—most horrifically—carte blanche to torture and kill.

The U.S. Air Force facility Area 51 is the source of many UFO conspiracy theories. Guarded in the highly classified secrecy of the CIA, many people think that Area 51 is home to extraterrestrial activity. Conspiracy theories suggest that alien autopsies are conducted at the site. Many people also believe that crashed alien spacecraft is examined at the site due—in part—to the Roswell incident in which weather balloon debris was thought to be that of a flying saucer. To this day, many people believe that the truth was covered up by the government.

With all of the corruption we've seen thus far, one has to wonder, how far will they go? It's easy to envision a "Big Brother"-like totalitarian state of government in which tyranny and fascism are normalized. This bleak dystopia sees government officials engaging in pervasive surveillance and human microchip implantation in their quest for omnipotence. When you dare to think for yourself, you pose a threat to the system. When you inspire others to think for themselves, you must be eliminated.

The government's mission is total control. They go to means of fraud, conspiracy, obstruction of justice, and countless unethical practices to attain that control. They classify information to protect themselves from lawsuits and any accountability, leaving them virtually untouchable. Their cold ambition gives way to depravity, ensuring immoral behavior. It's clear that most people don't know how to handle executive power; thus, corruption. Power is dangerous, be careful to whom you give it.

## *Wrong Trumps Right: Making America Hate Again*

He's a boisterous, contentious, grandstanding, political reality star. When Donald Trump decided to run for president, not many people thought he'd make it too far. People just thought it/he was a joke. What it turned out to be was a joke that went too far. The media—try as they might to defame him—is in large part responsible for his election. Through constant mention of his name, they promoted—almost celebrated—his ignorant behavior. It seemed that the more dirt they threw on his name, the more popular he became.

The impetus of his presidency—in my opinion—was born out of hatred and jealousy toward President Obama. Though he would die before he'd ever admit it, I wholeheartedly believe that a major part of Trump's political motivation came from seeing a respectable, intelligent, accomplished *Black* man leading this country. Even if Obama were a Conservative, I don't think his skin color could ever allow the presidency to be his *place* in Trump's mind. That's why Trump tried so hard to de-Americanize Obama through his "birther" campaign.

The election of Trump reflects how much America truly hates itself. America hates women, Black people, gay people, Jewish people, Muslims, foreigners, activists, conservationists, the poor, etc., but most of all, America hates equality. America hated itself enough to vote for a man who publicly mocked a disabled person—a man who thinks that his wealth and power entitle him to degrade and objectify women. Trump is America's ambassador of hate. A person like Donald Trump appeals to millions of White people who are basically tired of hiding their racism. They're tired of tip-toeing around Black people and having to suppress their first amendment right to express their hatred in favor of being politically correct. These people basically went out of their way to vote for hate, a disheartening portrait of the reprehensible state of our nation.

Trump wanted to "make America great again" and clean it up by getting rid of Muslims—or anyone who might look like a Muslim because they wear a "rag" on their head—spending the taxpayers' blue-collar earnings to build a wall that keeps out the "criminals" of Mexico, and defeating his nemesis, Obama, by eliminating healthcare for most of America. He wanted to prevent immigrants from "shithole countries" such as Haiti, El Salvador, and African countries from coming to America and, instead, have more immigrants from lily-White Norway. He wanted to take the American dream away from non-White immigrants—the same American dream that benefited previous generations of his family. These are the telltale words of the self-proclaimed "least racist person anybody is going to meet"—the same person who said "nobody has more respect for women than I do" after boasting about grabbing them "by the pussy."

During the 2016 election, Trump received a disturbing amount of support from White supremacist groups, including the Ku Klux Klan. He refused to denounce these hate groups, presumably in order to retain their support and to get their votes. He even re-tweeted a few quotes from some well-known racist dictators. Most of his campaign seemed to be based on a platform that promoted hate as a tactic to make America great again. These tactics included banning all Muslims from the country, and racially profiling Mexicans who—according to him—are "rapists" who bring "drugs" and "crime" into the country.

There were a number of cases of bigoted White Trump supporters attacking Black protestors. Trump himself seemed to be the catalyst behind these incidents as he glorified and even encouraged violence at his Klan-like rallies. With shameless race-baiting toward a mindless, hate-filled audience, the 2016 race was like a coming-out party to make a statement that it was okay to hate freely and publicly in order to "take back our country." Supporters of Trump live in an alternate reality of delusion and lawlessness, and Trump has normalized this type of behavior.

Late in his bid for presidency, Trump made a desperate, insulting attempt at gaining Black voters by asking, "What the hell do you have to lose?" Speaking—as usual—before an almost all-White crowd, he went on to generalize and degrade Black people by saying that our "schools are no good," that we're "living in poverty," and that if you walk down the streets in our neighborhoods, "you get shot." The only thing is, this time, he was actually trying to appeal to White people who genuinely care about Black people by pretending that he does as well.

For all of his offensive insensitivity, Trump maintained that sensitivity training for companies was "racist," and that those who implemented this practice were trying to make us "hate our country." Apparently, racism is so American that combating racial injustice means that you hate this country. Donald Trump and Mike Pence promoted the agenda that systemic racism doesn't exist because it benefits them, and they didn't want to have to do anything about it. Trump thrives off of racism. It's even alleged that he proposed a White people vs. Black people season of his former reality show, *The Apprentice.*

He compulsively contended that any media outlet that didn't agree with him was "fake news" and that every investigation or indictment cast against him was a "witch hunt." He preferred to deal exclusively with news organizations that indulged his ignorance, like Fox News. You could also count on him tweeting around the clock in constant defense of his own ego. This ego of his is so fragile and delusive that he had to go out of his way to assert that he defeated Hillary Clinton by a landslide, that he had the most-attended inauguration in history, and that he was in the best shape of any U.S. president ever, despite his obvious obesity and fast-food diet.

The odious former leader of our country—in reference to Syria—once proudly proclaimed "I would bomb the shit out of them." These words eerily recall those of a terrorist. Disturbingly enough, he proposed spending $54 billion to basically start another war as if he had nothing else to do. It's like he thought that he was playing make-believe with toy soldiers while acting as their dictator. To have his hands on the controller of his World of Warcraft was just a fun, casual way of flexing his power. For someone like Trump to have this kind of power is extremely dangerous. His every word and action depict those of a childish clown with orange skin and yellow hair—to match his yellow belly—who is overly determined to prove that he isn't a pussy. However, if money couldn't protect him, and if the Secret Service couldn't protect him, I'm pretty sure that he would have a lot less to say.

From *jokingly* telling cops to use more force when making arrests to his ban on Muslims and transgender people, Trump has proved to be a threat to the civil rights of all minorities and disenfranchised people. He has given the very strong impression that it's okay to target and profile these people and treat them with disrespect because they don't belong in his version of America. With the help of U.S. Immigration and Customs Enforcement (ICE), the Trump administration separated immigrant children from their parents and put them in cages over his *zero tolerance* policy for treating immigrants like human beings. He's made it clear that because of the actions of some, all Mexicans are "lowlifes," all Muslims are "evil," all Black men are "thugs," and transgender people aren't good enough to represent this country in the military.

Trump reached an inconceivable level of impunity where he could do everything wrong and not have to face any repercussions. He seemed virtually untouchable. The same energy that got him elected as president is the same energy that kept him in office, despite his glaring incompetence. Even multiple impeachment attempts couldn't remove him from office. To say that his performance as leader of the free world was disappointing would be redundant. Although, what's most disappointing to me is his lack of accountability and ownership. As bold and arrogant as he is—and with as much as he's gotten away with—he somehow is still afraid to admit to being a racist, elitist misogynist.

Some celebripublicans like to attach their name to his by showing their support—or by publicly agreeing with his views—all in an effort to bask in his residual spotlight. People like Roseanne Barr and Kanye West—who, in my opinion, have the same megalomaniacal complex as Trump—aligned themselves with him seemingly because they want what he has: power, wealth, and a constant media focus rooted in controversy. They seem to want the same attention that he receives for saying and doing the most morally contemptuous things without consequence.

People like these are conveniently blind to Trump's more inhumane views and self-serving agenda, always noting that he created more jobs and improved the economy. I guess if he makes the wealthy more wealthy, he doesn't have to treat people like people. They come up with the most ridiculous reasons for following him—"He was an outsider who beat the odds," "He's a good businessman," "He's unfiltered and entertaining," "If he can become president, there's hope for me"—completely ignoring the lack of integrity in his character. Trump showed America exactly who he is, and most Conservatives either chose to remain ignorant about it, or they were happy to know that he's just like them.

There are also many Conservatives who hate Trump, but kiss his ass in person. Mike Pence—Trump's former VP sidekick who essentially became marked for death after Trump incited the Capitol coup—still maintained an obsequious allegiance to him despite Trump defending his Jan. 6 lynch mob's chanting of "hang Mike Pence." Like Pence, Trump's frenemies possess a willful stupidity in place of integrity. As long as Trump has power and influence, they're all too willing to continue blowing their *trump*ets to appease him.

The entire purpose of Trump's presidency was to feed his own ego. Besides all of the political firestorms he created to make himself feel tough, he also implemented the ridiculous Trumpy bear to rival President Roosevelt's Teddy bear. He even tried to have his hideous visage added to Mount Rushmore. In 2022, this outrageously overindulged child released a collection of digital trading cards with his head superimposed on—among other characters—a brawny superhero. It blows my mind that so many people eagerly follow someone so delusionally narcissistic. I wouldn't be surprised if there were a push toward a national holiday in his honor at some point.

After being banned from all major social media platforms, he launched the ironically-named Truth Social. The man who was found by fact-checkers to have made over 30,000 false statements during his term as president is clearly allergic to the truth. He proved to be a source of disinformation regarding mail-in voting and the Covid pandemic. His downplaying and mishandling of the coronavirus might have cost hundreds of thousands of lives. Leading by an unthinkably careless example, he continued to throw rallies while discouraging the use of face masks. In what initially seemed like poetic justice, he contracted the virus only to quickly recover and develop a false sense of immunity based on his own privilege.

Trump has proved to be as treasonous as he accused certain Black NFL players to be. At the 2018 Helsinki summit, he threw the U.S. Intelligence Committee under the bus out of subservient loyalty to Russian dictator Vladimir Putin, proving how spineless he truly is. Although, Trump's loyalty to Putin was perhaps his repayment for the collusion that influenced his 2016 election win.

When Trump lost his bid for reelection in 2020, he reacted exactly as expected: like a petulant child who had his toys taken away from him. He made baseless claims of voter fraud because—in his delusional mind—that was the only possible reason he could ever lose an election. He went on a temper tantrum tour, throwing rallies, filing failed lawsuits, issuing corrupt pardons, and further proving why he was a pathetic excuse for a leader. Being the sore loser that he is, he refused to attend the inauguration of his successor—President Biden—and clung pitifully to the idea of overturning the election results. Of course, he ranted incessantly on social media and—at a rally on January 6, 2021—commanded his "proud boys" to storm the Capitol on his behalf. He emboldened these terrorists to do his dirty work, many of whom didn't even care enough to vote for him.

It wasn't until after he incited the Capitol insurrection that he was finally banned on all major social media platforms, including his favorite soap box, Twitter (X). After years of reckless, irresponsible posts, why did it take so long to silence him? Why did they have to wait for a deadly act of domestic terrorism to take place before they took action? More importantly, what kind of president wages war on his own country?—The only U.S. president to be impeached twice.—The only U.S. president to be indicted on criminal charges.—A criminal, a fraud, and the absolute worst president in U.S. history.

It was President Lincoln who said, "If you want to test a man's character, give him power." The power of the presidency definitely magnified the despicable character of Trump. My worry is that—with his careless behavior—he's molded a new precedent for Republican candidates to come. The Trump presidency was an unfathomable display of corruption and impunity. The word *great* died in the presidential office fof Donald J. Trump.

### *Freedom of Silence: The Contradiction of Being Politically Correct*

Freedom of speech, apparently, isn't free. Our first amendment right seems to be our right to remain silent. In today's world, everything is political; thus, everything is required to be politically correct. This notion draws complaints from many racists, classists, and sexists who don't like to be called out for their prejudiced views. They argue that the progression of political correctness robs them of their freedom of speech. I disagree.

Freedom of speech is self-defining in every case as the right to speak freely about whatever you choose—whenever you choose—in spite of what's deemed politically correct. However, what people need to understand is that while they're entitled to their own opinions, everyone else is entitled to their own reaction to those opinions. If you're bold enough to put it out there, you have to take what comes with it. Freedom of speech doesn't mean freedom from consequences.

Because of today's cancel culture, people run the risk of being cancelled for almost anything they do or say. That being said, not every cancellation is about cancel culture; it's about accountability. As times continue to change, certain speech and behaviors that were once accepted are no longer tolerated and have to be corrected when they are observed—this has been referred to as corrective evolution. As a result, a lot of people have had their past social media posts come back to haunt them years later.

There's always another someone who is fired or forced to resign due to backlash from their past posts, which makes me wonder, where do we draw the line? At some point in our lives, we've all said or done something insensitive and inappropriate, even if we weren't dumb enough to post it online. Is it fair to automatically condemn someone for who they used to be? Is there a statute of limitations on how far back that judgment can extend? People are silenced and banned on social platforms all of the time, but that contradicts their freedom of speech. Is it unconstitutional to ban—or shadow ban—people on social media, or is it a situational necessity?

In 2022, psycho-eccentric tech billionaire Elon Musk purchased Twitter to attain the power of preserving free (hate) speech on social media. Almost immediately, he got rid of most of the staff who presumably stood in the way of his agenda—which would ultimately be revealed through the rebranding to X—and unfiltered, uncensored, hateful rhetoric resurged with a vengeance. All of the Twitter trolls came out—like roaches in the dark—to exercise their right to vomit putrid malevolence into cyberspace. Well, at least they exposed themselves as the bigoted racists they are, and are vulnerable to the consequences thereof.

Ours is a country obsessed with race. Some people (maybe you) have a compulsive need to make racial jokes. If others are offended by it, they're too sensitive—because everyone has to find your racist humor hilarious. Yet, somehow, you're *not* racist; you just enjoy making stereotypical observations at the expense of other races and not your own. I wonder how many people would be openly racist if doing so didn't have financial or social implications?

I've noticed that a lot of people like to push their personal agendas with propaganda like bumper stickers and vanity license plates. Too many of us are so full of ourselves that we actually think everyone cares about our petty views. People like to take freedom of speech to the extreme. They feel like their right to this freedom gives them license to advertise hate speech and disrespect. The hardest thing about freedom of speech is accepting other people's right to it as well.

Many of us are insensitive about certain things because they don't directly relate to us. It's easy to be politically incorrect when you have a politically biased viewpoint. So many people are desperately eager to spew irreverent rhetoric. They love to say that they're "brutally honest" because they believe that saying so makes it okay to be verbally abusive. Honesty doesn't require brutality, the truth is the truth. Just be brutally honest with yourself and admit that you're an asshole. It's not about political correctness, it's about respect. You can give your opinion without being disrespectful.

The over-censorship on TV and radio has gotten a bit ridiculous. What's the point of playing a song on the radio if you have to censor every other word?

Television networks are stuck in the habit of blurring—even simulated—nudity. As hard as it is to believe, censorship on the major TV networks was actually a lot milder in the '90s than it is today. On the sitcom *Roseanne*, they would say words like *dyke*, *lesbo*, and *butch*, but when episodes of the show air today, those words are often censored or edited out. There is definitely an oversensitivity these days that just didn't exist back then.

Are we too sensitive? Have we gone too far with cancel culture? Even if everything has gotten too politically correct, I think that we just have to deal with it. You can't realistically expect everyone to yield to your objections and tiptoe around your sensitivities, it's unreasonable. You also can't tell someone what—or what not—to be offended by. Just because it doesn't offend you doesn't mean that it shouldn't offend anyone else. Every person is different—isn't that why you make fun of them in the first place?

## *God, Guns & Greed: The Conservative Cult*

God, guns, and greed are each a source of power. The good ol' people of the GOP use all three as weapons against democracy. For Conservatives, insatiable is their pursuit of power.

They worship at the altar of their lord and savior Donald Trump, whom they defend obsequiously. They make excuses for his prejudice and incompetence, and are more than willing to make themselves look foolish by adopting his delusion. With Trump, they know that rules don't apply, facts don't matter, and reality becomes whatever figment they choose to imagine. These conservative Karens go on the warpath to promote his "fake news" agenda. They even concocted the ridiculous diagnosis of "Trump Derangement Syndrome" for anyone who calls him out on his bullshit. Ironically, this diagnosis is much better suited to Trump and his mindless "Trumpers." Their allegiance isn't to the GOP or to America, everything they do seems to be an effort to please him. The GOP has become a hate group—a cult of acolytes for Trump.

They're fueled by their flag bearers on the partisan platform of Fox News, which basically encourages and promotes racism through hateful rhetoric. They obsessively reference Liberals and "the left" as their mortal enemy, denigrating them with childish insults like "Lib-tards." They seem to live for the thrill of this feckless war with Democrats. However, the enemy of Conservatives isn't Liberals, it's truth. They've created this fictitious world of alternative facts so that they can escape from—and not be held accountable for—the truth. Reality is negotiable in Conservatism. It's like a twilight zone where delusion has become contagion. This convenient delusion means that they don't have to accept truth—or anything associated with reality—if they don't agree with it.

Partisan apps like Truth Social and Parler are their platforms for shitting out alternative facts, bitching about "fake news," and crafting conspiracy theories. These apps are their safe haven for hate speech, which they use to pander to their demographic. They promote the idea that not having conservative ideals is "un-American." Their slogan seems to be, "If you don't hate what we hate, then you don't love America." For the most part, their psycho-conservative vitriol falls short of an outright admission of racism. For as bold as they pretend to be, they always seem to veil their hateful prejudice with conservative pretense.

The election of President Obama—America's first Black president—was the impetus of the bigoted Trumpism that has come to define Conservative politics. When Obama became president, Conservatives wanted him to fail as our leader, even at the expense of the country in which they and their families live. Conservatives are the niggards in opposition to the niggers. They're the majority who oppose the minorities—the power as opposed to the "weak." Conservatives always claim that the system is rigged when they can't manage to rig it in their favor. Unless they're in power, they want there to be crime and violence. They want to scare everyone with the threat of rapists, pedophiles, and murderers because it benefits them.

The Conservative cult blindly follows to the right of every political issue. Many Conservative women feign supercilious empowerment while under the thumb of an empowered Conservative man whom they are desperate to impress. Meanwhile, Conservative men seem to have a befuddling obsession with making a woman's biological choices for them. They live and breathe for the power of denying a woman's right to an abortion, even in cases of rape, incest, and risk to the life of the mother. I'm sure they'll have a temporary change of heart when their wives or daughters get raped and impregnated.

Conservative judgment begets judgment. In my eyes, they look like the most hateful, spiteful, malevolent people on Earth. The only thing that seems to make them happy in life is a political win. They don't seem to have any capacity for love and compassion. They use God as their self-righteous armor to condemn others while excusing themselves. They believe that the guise of Christianity is their license to cast judgment. Somehow, they're unaware that the objective of Christianity is to be Christ-like, which goes against almost everything they represent. Christ was an immigrant and also a philanthropist who served the disenfranchised with humility, while Conservatives frequently exhibit behaviors of xenophobia and classism.

Most Conservatives look down on the fast-food workers and waiters of the world, shaming these human beings for not having the lucrative corporate careers that they have. However—in actuality—they don't want these blue-collar individuals on their playing field because then they'd have no one upon whom to look down. Conservatives don't believe in equality, they believe in classism. These miserable misers don't take pleasure in their wealth, they take pleasure in other people's destitution, and they see it as their duty to make sure that these people know just how inferior they are.

It's quite apparent that Conservatives are against any aberration from their bigoted tradition, that's why they despise those whom they perceive to be "social justice warriors," like antifa. They fight fiendishly to protect their bigotry against civil rights and human decency, eager to further oppress disenfranchised minorities and sympathizers alike. As Conservatives fail in their roles of leadership or have incidents of controversy, they commonly create distractions to shift the pressure to the left instead of taking accountability. They generally have no tact or civility as evidenced by how comfortable they are at utilizing every racist trope and divisive device.

Conservatives hate the word *woke* because most of them would rather remain hibernated. They have no idea what the word actually means in relation to civil rights, so they've created their own meaning for it. To them, "woke" is basically anything that poses a threat to White supremacy. Conservatives are also deathly afraid of critical race theory because they don't want their children to know about the evil truths of American tradition. They're determined to whitewash history and keep America in the darkness of delusion—a delusion they've managed to normalize. They counter critical race theory with the ridiculous "replacement theory," which—with paranoid absurdity—insists that White people are being replaced by non-White people through some sort of "genocide by substitution." This theory is yet another convoluted reason for them to spread hate and incite racist action.

America's Conservative Klansmen lead by fear and hate. They use fear to provoke their followers to hate their opposition. They project their own hate onto Liberals by claiming that Liberals hate America. However, if Conservatives hate Liberals as well as foreigners, Black people, Jewish people, gay people, and women, then *they* hate America. It's these same jingoistic Conservatives who heroize the Capitol insurrection as a patriotic act of duty, thereby condoning domestic terrorism. They'll always use politics to justify their violence while hypocritically condemning the "thugs" they hear about in the news and on social media. They seem to have a primitive bloodlust, leaving them with no regard for the lives of those who don't share their misguided convictions.

This new era of radical far-right extremists includes Trump's Capitol-storming Proud Boys, the disturbingly delusional QAnon cult, the Oath Keepers, the 3 Percenters, and the White nationalist Nazis of the alternative right. The alt-right are admittedly racist for the sake of the "biological survival" of the White race. They whine constantly about losing their rights as White men. They're so full of hate and vitriol that their countenance is gnarled in an ugly, demonic perma-scowl. They're so afraid of equality, they're panic-stricken. What they don't realize is that racism is an infection of insecurity. If your superiority keeps you in power, then why are you worried about Black people and foreigners taking that away from you? Besides, if it can be taken away, it isn't true power.

Conservatives often substitute the American flag for the "thin blue line" flag—a flag that is said to represent support for law enforcement, but actually has come to represent division and White supremacy. They use false patriotism to simultaneously veil and flaunt their racism. They use politics to justify hate. Their flags—along with lawn signs, window stickers, bumper stickers, and other political propaganda—serve to advertise their racist agenda. Why does being a "red-blooded American" mean being a red pill-swallowing, bigoted, bellicose psycho-nationalist? Why doesn't conservative American pride evoke happiness?

Because of their obsession with guns, most Conservative people love to hunt. Camouflage has become the far-right uniform. Conservatives are also notoriously pro-war. To me, it all seems to be about the thrill of the kill. Hunting in the woods and fighting in the war allow them to kill legally. They use the justification of helping to "control the wildlife population," and serving to "honor thy country," but it's all about asserting their power by taking lives.

Conservatives have a steadfast resistance to gun control laws. The right to bear arms is crucial to their principle of power, but what if more of the Black male demographic gained permits and attained firearms legally? I imagine Conservatives would then insist on gun control laws just so they could regain an advantage. To them, when a Black man carries a gun, he's a criminal, but when a White man carries a gun, he's an American. How is it that Conservatives are pro-life *and* pro-guns? They can kill wild animals, trespassers, and "thugs," but only abortion is deemed morally wrong? Their entire belief system is riddled with convenient contradictions. The Bible says, "Thou shall not kill;" there's no subtext and no asterisks, so there should be no excuses or justification.

Every year, there are dozens of mass shootings in America. When these attacks occur, NRA-funded politicians and law makers only seem to offer the same "thoughts and prayers" and insincere "condolences" instead of logical ideas on how to prevent future attacks and put an end to this horrendous cycle of gun violence. Their idea for handling gun violence in schools is to arm the teachers, which would—of course—solve everything. So, now, teachers are expected to double as security guards for the same low pay? It only makes sense in a conservative mind.

After the Parkland tragedy in February of 2018, students and protestors organized the March for Our Lives demonstration for gun control legislation. Viewing this as an attack on their right to kill, Conservatives pushed back, often with immature and heartless tweets aimed at teenage victims of gun violence. The fact that conservative politics seems to be more important than the lives and safety of these innocent teenagers is revolting. It seems like these mass shootings are just collateral damage in a much bigger war for Conservatives. The reason they fight so obsessively for maintaining gun rights is so that they can move comfortably throughout the community inciting hatred and anger with the hopes of having a reason to "defend themselves" with a firearm under a law that only protects *them*. For these proud Americans, the right to bear arms means the right to kill.

Southern Republicans seem to have a disturbing obsession with lynching. Texas Representative Chip Roy—during a congressional hearing on anti-Asian

American violence—gave his idea of "justice," which is to "find all the rope in Texas and get a tall oak tree" to take out the "bad guys." This hate-mongering rhetoric was taken from a country song by Toby Keith called "Beer for My Horses," in which he sings "round up all of them bad boys, hang them high in the street." Republican politics has always had a strong influence in the country music world. Many of these cowboy cowards use the "outlaw" image as a guise for their White supremacy.

In July 2023, country singer Jason Aldean released a video for his song "Try That in a Small Town," which was filmed in front of the Columbia, TN courthouse where a Black man, Henry Choate, was lynched in 1927. The video featured clips of Black Lives Matter (anti-police brutality) protests to spark the hateful interest of Sundown Town, USA. When CMT banned his video for its divisive content, Aldean embraced the opportunity to play victim on social media and gain the sympathy of his racist fans who immediately sent the song to number one on iTunes and eventually on the Billboard Hot 100. Like every other racist coward, he denied the true intent of the song—which was a clear threat to BLM—and in the end, he got exactly what he wanted. For the conservative Klan, hate sells.

Conservatives led the charge against Colin Kaepernick for choosing to kneel during the national anthem in protest of racial inequality and police brutality. They completely distorted his silent protest to make it about disrespecting the American flag so that they didn't have to address the real issue of injustice. They painted him as America's enemy, Trump even called him—and his fellow protestors—a "son of a bitch." They imposed a false narrative on the entire country which insisted that Kaepernick was anti-America, anti-police, and anti-military. Their claim that he was being disrespectful to our troops by not saluting the flag was a desperate reach. Besides, the stars and stripes is not the military's flag, it's the people's flag.

Because of the controversy caused by his take-a-knee movement, there were colluded efforts to have Kaepernick blacklisted from the NFL. They claimed that he brought unwanted attention to the league by mixing it with politics, but doesn't the singing of the national anthem at every game add politics to it? This is also a very hypocritical anthem with an omitted third verse that reads in part, "No refuge could save the hireling and slave from the terror of flight or the gloom of the grave." While this obviously contradicts America being the "land of the free," it is a banner for exactly what America thinks of its own people.

It is the steadfast mission of Republicans to suppress the votes of Black people—and other minorities—in hopes of enacting a new Jim Crow era. They use the "Southern strategy" of President Nixon and President Hoover to take advantage of racism through Jim Crow tactics. This new age Lily-White Movement hearkens back to the outright racism of the Reconstruction era. Conservative politicians fight to pass bills and change laws to support their prejudice. It just goes to show the lengths they'll go to "make America (White) again." Republican senators voted against making Juneteenth a national holiday, proclaiming there's "only one Independence Day." That sentiment says it all. Black people weren't free when the Declaration of Independence was signed, and—to Conservatives—our freedom doesn't matter.

In September 2021, civil rights activist Rev. Al Sharpton visited Del Rio, TX to speak on Haitian migrant mistreatment at the hands of U.S. Border Patrol. These agents on horseback—while swinging their horses' reins like whips—confronted Black migrants and corralled them like cattle. These disgusting images recalled times of slavery. While condemning this abuse, Sharpton was heckled by White Conservatives who attempted to attach their prejudice onto him by yelling "You're a racist. Nobody wants you in Texas." Conservatives claim that Black people create racism simply because we point it out.

Republican representatives fight tooth and nail for a border wall to keep immigrants from entering the country, but still hire them illegally for less than minimum wage. It is very apparent that most Conservatives have zero tolerance for those unlike them in regards to religion, sexuality, socioeconomic status, and race. They seem to have a strong belief that this country would be much better off without Muslims, Black people, Jewish people, Mexicans, gay people, and most women, so they tell us to hate them. However—because their lifestyle is rooted in hate—they absolutely need us minorities. If we weren't here, who would they hate? Would they really be happy then? Not likely.

There was a time when Conservatives—like the Reagans—had some level of dignity and class. Today's Conservatives are shameless extremists. Most of the new Conservatives are former Liberals who used to stand up against one-percenter capitalists, now their political opposition is racially motivated. Many of these same people were against police and their abuse of power until the police started killing Black people almost exclusively. Because of their gullible ignorance, these *blue*-collar Americans were brainwashed by the Grand Ol' Partisanship.

The colors that represent America are the red elephant, White supremacy, and the thin blue line. With God, guns, and greed as its tenets, bigotry and evil dwell deep in the Conservative cult.

FABIAN M.C. KUYKENDALL

### *For the Love of War: The "Collateral" Damage of Government Interest*

It's been said that war is conceived from religion, but war is actually conceived from the religion of politics. Everyone has a different idea of how their country should be ran, and any opposition to this—or a general distaste for government—leads to war. It's evident that most people are religiously devoted to all things political. They dedicate all of their time, effort, and energy to fight against those who disagree with their views. No matter how miserable it makes them, people are more than willing to serve their political gods at the expense of their own contentment.

The truth—as I see it—is that most people don't want peace. For them, there's more honor and ego fulfillment in war. In America, we're programmed to believe that if we love our country, we should risk our lives to protect the rich and privileged citizens who are too important to do the same. Even with his obsessive celebration of war, I am most certain that Donald Trump would never—at any age—go to war for this country. I'm sure it was much easier for him to send thousands of men and women overseas to die or lose limbs in order to protect *his* freedom and his cushy lifestyle. All the while, he sat in the highest elected office with his finger on the button of nuclear war.

The military and the government want you to believe that serving your country means dedicating and risking your life to fight a war. Meanwhile, millions of us working-class Americans serve our country every day by giving our labor, and for our service, we get the honor of having our paychecks raped by the government. This same government brainwashes its troops to value government interest over their own lives and families. America's national anthem is a war song, which speaks volumes about our values. We're taught that to show love, we must express hate, but loving your country shouldn't mean starting a war with the rest of the world.

Many people want a justifiable reason to kill and destroy, and any accolades or celebrity they receive as a result of that is just icing on the cake. I believe that the praise we bestow upon soldiers only condones and glorifies war. It even seems that most soldiers, veterans, and police officers have an expectation of praise, and—for many of them—that's the main reason why they serve. They're indifferently desensitized to taking lives because killing is glorified. Many young boys dream of one day being on a SWAT or SEAL team simply for the glory of the kill.

Military veterans are honored and thanked for their service all of the time, yet the same government that honors them publicly, allows them to return to destitution and undertreated PTSD after they've fulfilled their duty. Many immigrant veterans have been deported for misdemeanors that would have only given natural-born citizens a slap on the wrist. These immigrants are good enough to fight for our country, but, apparently, not good enough to live in it. Our contradictory government seems to only see its soldiers as expendable pawns in their international game of chess.

Many people say that we're in the midst of a civil war here in the United States. Aside from the incessant political battles, there are mass shootings almost every week. There are hate crimes that verge on terrorism, and there's the steady tension of a nation on the brink of an anarchic purge. If we were to be invaded by terrorists from overseas, we would redirect our hateful energy away from each other and toward them. Ironically, it seems that war is the only thing that can bring us together as a nation.

Putin's war with Ukraine showed how desperate he was to prove his dick size or overcompensate for it. Trying to destroy Ukraine to make Russia look powerful only proved how weak Russia truly is. These cowardly Russian troops committed unthinkable war crimes against Ukrainians including torture, rape, and genocide. This senseless "war of aggression" was a failed power grab, which left widespread "collateral" damage in the form of innocent lives.

Wars like this are narcissistic displays of evil for imperialism. Evil equals immortality, that's why people will forever mention a certain Nazi dictator. Whether they're satirizing him in media or just speaking his name, they're celebrating him. They're celebrating evil. I'll never understand how people can be so anesthetized to the atrocities of war and have such a callous disregard for human life.

Is war a necessary evil? Soul legend Marvin Gaye told us that "war is not the answer, for only love can conquer hate." War is a crime against humanity as innocent civilians ultimately pay the price. I wonder how many government leaders are willing to fight their own wars and die for us?

## *The Uncivil War: America's Political Schism*

Politics centers around division. In America, we're expected to pledge allegiance to a Republican or Democratic party by swallowing either a red or blue pill. Being an American citizen comes down to being left or right, Black or White, wrong or right. Politics is what happens when we're not evolved enough as a civilization to be civil.

Each side seems to care more about winning than making a positive change. We treat each other like foreign enemies of war instead of like fellow American citizens. We can't call ourselves true patriots if we'd rather let our country implode by going to war with each other than to compromise and make peace for the betterment of our nation. We make every human issue a Conservative/ Liberal issue. We politicize non-political issues so that we can gather the masses to join in our spiteful opposition. Everything has to be a contest to gain some shallow victory. We love choosing sides, so we balkanize every situation to act on our bloodlust. We politicize to polarize.

Americans use politics as a license to fight and to hate. We treat elections like sports events in which we root for our favorite team instead of realizing the magnitude of what's at stake. Being American means engaging in its ever-growing list of culture wars. This country is infested with political narcissists battling over what should define America. The news media force-feeds us political ads and propaganda during every election period. They even hijack video-sharing platforms like YouTube, making sure that no one can escape the relentless political migraine.

Our is a Congress of many incompetent men and women who act and react with biased emotion instead of honest patriotic duty. During the second impeachment trial of Donald Trump, the Republican Senate remained spinelessly devoted to him instead of the country they're supposed to serve—because if they had done their job and voted to convict him, that would have given a victory to their evil nemeses, the Democrats. Somehow, this immoral partisanship took precedence over holding Trump accountable for inciting an act of domestic terrorism that claimed several lives. This implicit bias on behalf of our Senate is dangerous and disgraceful. They have zero integrity, sacrificing their souls to make sure that Trump gets away with murder.

Even previous opponents of Donald Trump like former New Jersey Governor Chris Christie and former House Speaker Paul Ryan—who categorically disagreed with Trump's beliefs—decided to back his bid for presidency. Apparently, GOP loyalty is more important than what's best for this country. It's amazing how willing they were to overlook his questionable qualifications and his obvious self-serving agenda just for the opportunity to celebrate a win for their Grand Ol' Party.

The presidency used to be a noble responsibility, now it's an ego-driven power grab. Every candidate for political office has the same forced sincerity and covert agenda, and they follow the same fake political script of "I approve this message because I wrote it." Politicians and analysts alike have resorted to attempts at justifying their clouded views with the use of alternative facts, which is just another phrase for outright lies. When you don't vote, they say that you're not using your voice or fulfilling your civic duty, but they only want you to vote for *their* benefit.

Also, there are too many people who vote just for the right to complain. Everyone—from politicians to blue-collar citizens—seems to think that they know what's best for this country, and they aren't willing to compromise or just agree to disagree. In some selfish state of delusion, they expect everyone to think and act as *they* do. The disagreement between both parties has become so hostile and aggressive. Politicians are supposed to represent America with—at the very least—professionalism instead of fanning the flames of toxic division.

Morals don't seem to matter anymore, whether conservative or liberal. Most Americans vote for candidates based solely on which party they represent. It's ridiculous to believe that one could wholeheartedly agree with every political view of one party. Unfortunately, there are many politicos and citizens who place partisanship over integrity. These are the morally irresponsible individuals who, when presented with facts from the opposition—which they clearly understand and sometimes even agree with—still choose to side with their own party instead of thinking for themselves and enlightening their party about what's morally right. Every election ultimately comes down to choosing the lesser of two evils.

Politics is a lot like religion with each party representing a different denomination. Many disciples of the political religion are mindless followers who devote their lives to serving their shepherd with blind faith. There aren't enough independent thinkers in this country, that's why we've never elected an independent president. The vast majority of us are cattle that are willingly herded to one side or the other. We are not a democracy. We elect politicians to make decisions on our behalf. They think for us and they act for us; therefore, we have no voice. Therein lies the hypocrisy of democracy.

There's far too much corporate interest and influence involved in politics. Mega-companies like Facebook and Twitter (X) shouldn't be giving politicians a platform to spread hate and misinformation for the sake of influencing—or manipulating—an election. There are countless corporations that donate billions of dollars lobbying to Congress and presidential campaigns. When money buys power, there's obvious corruption.

I have an unpalatable distaste for politics. I am not a Republican. I am not a Democrat. I am a person. If your life needs politics, you can have it; I'd rather have my sanity. The world of politics is miserable and exhausting. No politician is truly happy, and they never will be. Most of them seem to be destined for an emotional breakdown, yet, somehow, the mentally unstable manage to thrive in the political world.

Ours is a country of deep division. Our sad need to indulge in hateful politics—and our refusal to unite and get over our differences—will be to our own detriment. Too many of us want this division to escalate into the next civil war to take out our frustrations, to release our aggressions, to make someone pay for not giving us our way. Why can't we be civilized—or just civil? Nobody wins in a civil war.

# CHAPTER 4 - RELIGION & SPIRITUALITY

*Secular Theology: The Hypocrisy of Organized Religion*

So many saints of sanctimony use religion to justify their iniquities. They believe that their religion entitles them to a self-righteousness, which allows them to speak for God and decide whom He loves and whom He hates. They weaponize religion by using it as a license to judge, and they politicize religion by using it as a campaign to create division. Their mentality is, "I can do all things through Christ who entitles me."

People act as if God works exclusively for them and against everyone else. They use Him as their excuse and defense for almost everything. People also treat God like their own personal genie. They pray only to ask for trivial things as they prey upon His loving kindness. They convince themselves that God will forgive any and all of their sins, so they commit them freely. Essentially, people create their own religion, the doctrines of which they revise at their convenience.

Religion uses fear to control. Many denominations urge you to repent your sins and to obey God or be condemned to eternal hell. Are all sins created equal? It doesn't make sense that stealing a pack of gum and committing a murder would deserve the same punishment of burning in hell. In Catholicism, it's customary to confess your sins, but I don't understand the idea of confessing to a Catholic "father" in place of Father God. Moreover, I'm ill at ease about confessing sins to a priest when too many priests have taken away the innocence of young children with their own sins.

I feel that many—if not most—religious sects are Kool-Aid-drinking cults. I believe that these sects are in fact secular and that they use religion as a cover for immoral behavior. The Fundamentalist Church of Jesus Christ of Latter-Day Saints (FLDS) is a totalitarian polygamist cult posing as a Christian denomination. They condition their members to believe that giving in to their nefarious teachings is the only way to earn God's favor. Their former leader—Warren Jeffs—was sentenced to life in prison for his evil crimes within the walls of this cult. Jeffs—the so-called prophet of the church—married, raped, and impregnated dozens of underage girls to satisfy his sexual depravity under the guise of religion.

FLDS followers don't worship God, they worship their "prophet." This prophet and his cult leaders have concocted a system of beliefs to justify their sins. They assign multiple women and young girls to older men because "the more wives a man has, the closer he is to heaven." They practice incest to keep their "perfect bloodline" in tact and to avoid being tainted by "mud races." They also practice welfare fraud—which they refer to as "bleeding the beast"—to take advantage of what they see as a corrupt government. Their contradictory doctrines serve to keep their members brainwashed as their leaders indulge in a gluttonous feast of sex and power.

The Southern Baptist Convention has a long history of sexual misconduct among its leaders. They are often complicit in covering up allegations and resistant in addressing their culture of abuse. These demons in angels' robes use the name of Christ to take advantage of the lost and vulnerable, exploiting their need for purpose through religion. Their victims are often forced to get abortions after being impregnated from their assaults, which is completely hypocritical to the Southern Baptist pro-life stance.

Southern Baptists are strongly against comprehensive sex education, pornography, homosexuality, and fornication. They also have a strong opposition to critical race theory despite supposedly renouncing their past defense of slavery, segregation, and White supremacy. Also—for some reason—they forbid women from serving as pastors, even though they affirm that women are of equal value to men. Their whole belief system is smeared with religious right hypocrisy.

Muslim women seem to have no identity—as if they're just servants of the patriarchy. I don't understand why certain religions require their women to remain completely covered at all times. I also don't understand why the same rule doesn't apply to the men of said religions. From the outside looking in, it appears that such religious rules are only put in place to control women and to make them the property of the man. The fact that these women have to hide their feminine essence seems to suggest that there's something very wrong with being a woman.

It's astonishing how so many people fall for pseudoreligions like Scientology. Even with all of the reports and evidence of fraud, people still allow themselves to be completely brainwashed by pious criminals. Scientology is as much a business as it is a cult. It is built on ridiculous beliefs that ultimately use religion for mind control. Its principal purpose is profit, charging its members for expensive "auditing" in which Scientologists supposedly remove "engrams," or mental traumas. The Church of Scientology has been accused of organized harassment, psychological torture, espionage, human trafficking, forced labor, and violence against its members and those who oppose its pseudotheology. Perhaps we should ignore all of this since Tom Cruise is their poster child.

I don't understand why Christians have such a contradictory, antisemitic hatred toward Jewish people. As most people with an ounce of religious common sense know, Jesus was Jewish. Also—as the founder of Christianity—he was averse to hatred. It's shameful how many so-called Christians don't realize that the lesson in Christianity is to be Christ-like, yet some of those who do realize it still use Christianity to excuse their hateful, judgmental, and prejudiced ways.

Religion should not involve politics. Religious movements like Christian nationalism basically preach biased legislative ideas, which only seem to benefit White people. The Christian Identity sect—which is utter religious racism—has followers who've adopted the misguided belief that White people are the "chosen people," and that non-White people can never earn God's favor as they are soulless.

Was Jesus White? We know that he was Jewish and probably had Mediterranean features, but why would the savior of all mankind be specifically White? I feel like history's depiction and racial idealization of Jesus is the origin of the White savior complex. We're indoctrinated to worship a White Jesus, whereas veneration of The Black Nazarene is said to be idolatrous. It's unsettling to think of religion as a means to propagandize White supremacy.

Most religions follow a bible, but how holy is *the* Bible if it was written by sinners like me? We all were born into sin, so God doesn't fault us for not being faultless, but it's hard to believe in a religion whose Bible says that slaves should obey their masters and respect and fear them in the same way as they would Christ (Ephesians 6:5). It's hard to follow a Bible that was written—or rewritten—by racists. The Bible is like Wikipedia in that seemingly anyone can alter or add their own facts to it.

There's a lot that I don't understand about organized religion. I don't understand why people deify the pope—It's like they worship him as they do Christ. I also don't understand why so much of the irreligious influence has to be involved in religious things—I can't even tell the difference between gospel rap and secular rap. There was a time when people wore their "Sunday best" to every church service, now they dress as they would in a nightclub. Today, it's hard to distinguish heathens from puritans because they all seem to live the same way. There doesn't seem to be any stringent rules of religion; just worship God, but do as you please.

I don't subscribe to organized religion. I despise the hypocrisy of rich mega-church evangelists using church donations to support their lifestyle, pastors cursing in the house of the Lord during their sermons, ministers and clergymen using the church to commit their sex sins, and preachers not practicing what they preach. Most of today's church leaders seem to want God's glory for their own. They get a thrill out of pretending to be rock star celebrities in His name. God bless the faithful, but true faith has no room for sanctimonious pretense.

### *Fail Mary: Does Prayer Work?*

Prayer is central to religion. It is the spiritual line of communication that connects us to our higher power. For many of us, prayer is a daily ritual done before meals when we say grace and before we go to sleep at night. For others, prayer is done as an act of desperation in their darkest hour. Everyone seems to find religion in their time of need. We cry out to God when bad things happen to us, whether we believe in Him or not. It's very common for us to pray out of fear.

For most people, prayer involves asking for something instead of giving thanks. It always seems to be about acquiring what we don't have, not appreciating what we do have. Shamelessly, we pray for money, material possessions, sports wins, even good parking spots as opposed to good health and happiness for us and our loved ones. I believe that we abuse the privilege of the practice by praying for trivial things. Prayer is about personal spiritual communion, not telling your wish list to Santa.

People use prayer as a cure-all for intentional sins, almost like a spiritual Plan B pill. We lie, cheat, steal, and fornicate with the idea that praying afterwards will make it all okay. Some of us are even audacious enough to pray right before engaging in sinful behavior. Does prayer exonerate us from all sins? Is it really that simple? Does it forgive violence? Rape? Murder? It should go without saying that actively and purposely committing sins goes against living a life of righteous salvation, so how can we possibly use prayer as a justification?

Prayer is prevalent in sports from the players to the fans. There's even a well-known "Hail Mary" pass in football. Players often pray for strength or some kind of edge over their competition. When they succeed, they're fully convinced that it's because of a higher power—a secret weapon that makes them superior. I don't know if it's their higher power as much as it is their *faith* in that higher power that makes them victorious. Many of their fans—as a ritual of superstition—desperately pray for them to win. These fans provide a good example of steadfast faith; no matter how many times their team loses, they still remain loyal.

What do we expect from prayer—to get exactly what we pray for? Whatever higher power you have isn't going to fulfill your requests or grant your wishes just because you were kind enough to pray. Having these expectations only sets you up for disappointment. When our prayers aren't answered, we become disillusioned and tend to lose faith. This only highlights the fact that we're praying for the wrong reasons. It's been said that God helps those who help themselves. Therefore, praying isn't enough to get what we want; we also have to make an effort. They say that He may not come when you want Him, but He's always on time; that's why patience is a virtue. I think that it's best to let go of the burden of expectation, and pray to worship and give thanks, not receive it.

For me, prayer is how I communicate—as part of my spiritual relationship—with God. When I talk to God at night through prayer, I often feel like I'm begging or bothering Him by asking for things, even if I'm asking to be blessed with tomorrow. In the past, I've felt let down—even hurt—when it seemed like my prayers were in vain. It became too painful to ask for anything until I realized that God gives us what we need, not what we want. I've learned to make every prayer about expressing gratitude and not asking for things, but, instead, direction to acquire that which I need.

What is prayer to you? Is it magic? Is it just a futile ritual? Are we praying to an imaginary deity? Does it matter *how* we pray? Do we have to be on our knees, heads bowed, eyes closed with "praying hands?" Does it matter what we say when we pray? How long we pray? How hard we pray? What exactly do we have to do to make our prayers count? In the past, I've felt like I just wasn't doing it right—like I couldn't pray strong enough or well enough to be heard. I now know that I don't have to follow a praying template. I have a relationship with God that is tailored exclusively for me.

To believe in prayer, you have to believe in God or whatever you call your higher power. You have to have faith in that which can't be seen or explained. In other words, you have to believe in miracles. With every "Hail Mary" and "Our Father," it's our faith that makes us believe that our higher power will hear us, see us, and bless us. For many of us, prayer gives us hope. It's beyond a daily ritual or a religious obligation, it's essential to our spirit and our well-being. If the point of prayer is to make us feel better by giving us emotional reassurance, then I believe it does work.

## *Sin & Sentence: Defining Religious Morality*

The Bible says, "The wages of sin is death," but do we really have to pay the ultimate price for our sins? Being that we're born into sin, why would we be denied the paradise of Heaven in the afterlife on account of our sins? Is there a specific punishment for defying the Decalogue or committing any of the seven deadly sins? Many of us seek atonement for our sins, but to repent and be forgiven seems too easy. Does every sin deserve forgiveness?

If every transgression has a penalty, why do so many people seem to get away with murder, figuratively and literally? Not everyone seems to get the same karmic comeuppance for the same iniquities. It makes you wonder, what's the good in being good? As imperfect beings, can we ever be sanctified? In our quest for spiritual virtuousness, it seems like we're doomed to fail. In fact, it's getting harder to see the difference between the righteous and the wicked. Ultimately, no one really knows what's good and what's bad during our lifetime on Earth.

We use the Lord's name in vain by making God what we want Him to be. Like the many sanctimonious ministers who use spiritual manipulation for personal gain, we hide our sins behind His name. We create religions that insist that God condones our immoral behavior. We also make gods out of false idols by worshiping money, possessions, brands, celebrities, and other trivial things. This idle worship corrupts the world with soulless irreverence for that which is holy. Idolatry is so commonplace that many of us can't tell the sacred from the secular. Just like the mixing of worldly and gospel music, nothing is sacred anymore.

Every year, we see the blasphemy of people seeking attention for themselves on religious holidays. People make a living capitalizing on Christmas by appropriating the Santa Claus image or exploiting the holiday by making Christmas music solely for profit. Legendary singer Mariah Carey proclaimed herself the "Queen of Christmas" due to the annual record-breaking success of her Christmas music. If anyone deserves the title "Queen of Christmas," wouldn't it be Mary, mother of Christ? The holiday is supposed to be a *holy* day, free of the worldly sins of pride and greed. It's shameful to witness the sacrilege of the sacred.

It often seems like there are no consequences for the impious evils of man. The godless desecration of the cross-burning iconoclast: What's their cross to bear for the cross they burn? The profane blasphemy of saints who curse in the church, steal from the church, and fornicate in the church: For their sacrilege, what's their sacrifice? We engage in debauchery and hedonism because we can't yield to God's will. When we so easily give in to temptation, we descend to the depravity of Sodom and Gomorrah. Our fate could see each of us like a pillar of salt staring frozenly at infernal destruction.

The world is full of heresy from atheism to devil worship and demonology. It's amazing how many people subscribe to such sacrilegious dogmata. There are an untold number of underground pagans who conduct Black Mass ceremonies, perform Black Sabbath rituals, and engage in the black magic of the occult. The Satanists and antichrists of this netherworld willingly sell their souls to darkness. What's to become of them in the afterlife? Does God's love and forgiveness extend to those who deliberately choose evil over goodness?

We're overwhelmingly fortunate to receive God's mercy in lieu of His vengeance, especially when He could easily banish us to perdition. It's often said that God knows our hearts, which means He understands our intentions when we fall short of His glory. Inevitably, we all sin. However, it seems like we also have to pay for the world's sins; perhaps that's why bad things happen to good people. How do we combat the sins of others? If we can't fight fire with fire—and if two wrongs don't make a right—is there such a thing as a necessary sin?

We can't be expected to live free of sin. As hard as we try to live lives of virtue, it seems like everything we enjoy is sinful. If lust is a sin, can we love God and still love sex? If gluttony is a sin, is it wrong to indulge in the consumption of food? They say that you're not supposed to question God, but is it a sin to exercise the free will that God gave us? Nothing in life is fair, but the wages of sin are, indeed, necessary. We ultimately get what we deserve in life. Only a special kind of evil deserves the final judgment of Hell. Idealistically, I believe that Heaven is the reward for a life well-lived.

### *Superstition: What is Religion?*

While I don't necessarily consider myself a religious person, I do have a spiritual relationship with God. Although I often hear other people speak of being "more spiritual than religious," I rarely hear them mention a personal relationship with God. Many people substitute God with "the universe" in regards to spirituality and philosophy. They feel like they have to side with either God or the universe, religion or science, God or evolution.

Is man a concept of God, or is God a concept of man? Religion says that God created man, but if man created religion, is it plausible that he also conceived the notion of God? Can God be all good *and* all powerful? We're taught that God is good, but we've also heard Bible stories of how God uses His power when he gets angry. Is the Bible just a book of fairytales? The story of Christ is so beautifully miraculous that we want it to be true, but how can we distinguish it from fiction? Most people look to religion for answers, but there always seems to be more questions.

At some point in your religious walk, you have to stop and ask yourself, "Why do I believe?" Believing in that which you cannot see makes it merely a choice—a choice based on something personal instead of something tangible. There's no tangible reason to believe in superstition, yet many people do. To me, religion and superstition can seem interchangeable, but sometimes you have to cling to whatever works for you.

Superstition is said to be an irrational belief in the magical effects of an action or ritual. By that definition, praying would appear to be a superstitious act. People often pray for miracles, expecting the impossible. Superstition is like religion in that it involves irrational belief. It's superstitious to think that if you don't believe in God, you will end up in Hell. Is our final destination determined by our religious belief, or is it the same for everyone?

Religion is said to be a system of beliefs and practices relating to the divine. It's also said to be an obsession, something that someone is completely devoted to. It loses it's value when it's used to define trivial things like shopping, sports, and politics. Religion is a learned way of life, things that we were taught and to which we've grown accustomed. From the beginning, we're given opinions until we form our own.

Spirituality is said to be a system of belief that emphasizes the spiritual nature of existence. Many people appropriate spiritual lifestyles in what seems like a thirsty attempt at a personality makeover. I don't understand the pescatarian hypocrisy of not eating meat, but still consuming fish. A lot of people seem to think that their veganism gives them spiritual righteousness. You can't fake spirituality. Following a practice that doesn't align with who you are spiritually will ultimately be ineffective. There's no need for spirituality just for the sake of being spiritual.

Why do people worship? People are desperate for purpose. Some go to psycho-religious or psycho-political extremes in hopes to find that purpose. We need to believe that something bigger than us—an energy, a deity—is out there watching over us and guiding us to deliverance. Prayer and faith give us comfort, even when our prayers aren't answered. We have hope when our lives seem to be falling apart, that's why it's worth relying on blind faith.

I think that atheists actually do believe in God, they just don't want to. They've experienced terrible things in life, which made them upset with God to the point of questioning His existence. They're likely to be the ones who say, "If God loves me, then why does He let bad things happen to me?" I don't necessarily view them as pagans or even agnostics. I believe that they are freethinking souls who are just trying to find their way.

Many religions today don't involve a proverbial holy God. A lot of people reference the universe as their higher power. I think that this has a lot to do with the hypocrisy of organized religion and people's need for a more customized system of beliefs by which to live their lives. Buddhism is non-theistic and is a philosophy as much as it is a religion. Generally speaking, it seems that people tend to subscribe to the religion of spirituality. It gives us a connection to transcendental energy and a purpose for our lives.

Our perfect universe filled with perfectly-developed beings reminds me of why I believe in God. I don't think that the universe could create itself and continue to flourish for billions of years. I believe that we are able to see the face of God in nature, art, and in the innocent faces of children. My belief in God—and the proof of His existence—is in the beauty of His creations. For me, science is not a good enough explanation for the universe. Some creatures and creations are so perfect that only God could create them.

I've never seen God, but I've felt His energy. I've felt His protection and guidance when I was in harm's way. I know in my heart that I wouldn't have survived certain situations without His divine intervention. Though I don't subscribe to organized religion, I've developed my own personal relationship with God because that's what religion is to me. Religion is that which you choose to believe.

# CHAPTER 5 - PHILOSOPHY & THEORY

*Repelling From Gravity: The Power of Independent Thought*

Most people think that you're either a realist or an idealist. I'm pretty tall, so I believe that it's possible to simultaneously have my feet on the ground and my head in the clouds. I like to think of myself as an idealistic realist. I'm also an Aquarian—and it's been said that Aquarians are contrarians—so we tend to go left when everyone else goes right. It's all about thinking freely and not just accepting what's considered to be normal.

While it's hard to believe in that which is unseen, it stands to reason that there is life outside of Earth. It's been said that there are more stars and planets in the universe than grains of sand here on Earth. Among infinite worlds in space, why would ours be the only one to contain intelligent life? We're definitely not alone. There are aliens out there, but not necessarily the stereotypical skinny, green, bulb-headed, bug-eyed creatures that are often illustrated in film. These aliens could even be human like us. They're extraterrestrial and—to them—so are we.

While I don't necessarily believe in the idea of ghosts or spirits, I do believe in transcendental energy. I remain very skeptical of spiritual mediums, however. The demonization of ghosts and spirits has created—for many people—a paranormal paranoia. I believe that an evil spirit—or dark energy—only exists when you invite it. If you never experience the supernatural, can it really exist? I believe in angels because I choose to believe. I believe that there's life, there's death, and there's that in between.

A lot of people subscribe to the idea of reincarnation and multiple lifetimes. Have we experienced life countless times before now? Will we continue to live different life cycles indefinitely? What if we had several lifetimes which we were able to recall during our present one? What if we knew that we would have another lifetime after this one ended? Would we be tempted to start all over by committing suicide? Is death just an eternal out-of-body experience—an extrasensory perception of one's lifetime?

Philosophy creates existential crises that make everything seem futile. It makes us think that nothing is real; therefore, nothing matters. We ask ourselves, "What am I here for?" Many of us also experience death anxiety when our thoughts force us to face our mortality. When we live in fear of death, we die every day. It's those of us who are able to think freely who have philosophical breakthroughs in these moments of emotional breakdowns. When you can sit in your thoughts through deep meditation, you can answer your own questions and create your own purpose.

I believe that we are all specifically predestined, and I also believe that we have a hand in choosing our destiny. We determine our lives with our actions and how we respond to that which we can't control. We create our own essence as we are free-willed. I believe that we have to earn life as we live it. It is our life's mission to serve humanity with our unique calling. We all walk our own paths. Since everyone's path is so different, what is the meaning of life? That's a question to which only you can respond.

The film *A Clockwork Orange* is said to be based on the idea that humans innately have a sense of good and evil, and to deny their expression of either trait is to repress their human nature. I view this as a disturbing attempt to justify contemptible criminal behavior. Evil only exists so that we can appreciate that which is good. While we innately have a sense of both, we also have the will to choose between the two. For most people, it's easier to choose bad over good; it's also more fun. However, good is good and it's more rewarding. It's our will to abstain from the bad and evil that determines the quality of person we are.

Too many people seem to confuse science with philosophy as they attempt to turn personal opinions into scientific facts. So-called scientific research has found that a person's beauty lies within the symmetry of their face. Therefore, the more symmetric one's facial features are, the more attractive they appear. I find this—or any notion of scientific beauty—to be utterly ridiculous. Even as a man, I've been told that I'm beautiful, and my face is definitely lacking in symmetry. The point is, such a conclusion should not be drawn from something that is so subjective. Besides, philosophy tells us that beauty is in the eye of the beholder.

Philosophers often ask, "How can you truly know anything?" You can't. Can you? How can you *know* that you know? French Philosopher René Descartes famously declared, "I think, therefore I am." He believed that perfect knowledge required no doubt whatsoever. However, knowing and believing something doesn't necessarily make it true. Existence is a perpetual cycle of mutually contradictory questions and answers. No rhetorical question demands a rhetorical retort.

Some people still like to believe that Earth is flat just for the sake of challenging a fact. It's good to have a nonconformist mindset, but independent thought loses its power when we refuse to accept that which is proven to be factual. We can create our own philosophy, but it must revolve around the concept of truth. With reason, we can challenge theories, and with innovation, we can break new ground. The greatest advances in life are made with independent thought.

### *Intents & Purposes: Epistemology From an Abstract Perspective*

In my mind, there is often a battle of epistemic ambivalence. I find myself in deep rumination, pondering aimlessly for long periods of time. My train of thought is often derailed or shifted onto another track. Like many things in life, knowledge isn't a destination, it's a journey. We can never know everything, but what we don't know is just as important as what we do know.

Imagine if you were alone in your home and had the ability to hear the vocalization and movement of the hundreds or thousands of unseen insects that occupy your residence. What would that sound like? I imagine the noise would be a deafening drone—a frenetic cacophony of static that would send you into a state of psychosis. It's a bit unsettling to know that this noise actually does exist in our homes, we just can't hear it.

Imagine if you could feel every hair on your body as it grows. What would that feel like? To have such an acute sensory awareness might either be empowering or maddening. What if you could enhance one of your five senses at the expense of another, which would you choose? Imagine if synesthesia allowed you to taste colors or to hear shapes. This interplay between the senses would be perceptual stimulation, just inches away from sensory overload.

Do plants have feelings? I know that all vegetation and flora are alive, but how *aware* are they? If a tree falls in the woods ... does it feel pain? Many scientists say that plants feel pain and stress, and they react by folding their leaves or changing their appearance. Plants exhale the air that we need to breathe, which—in a way—anthropomorphizes them. They perspire, urinate, defecate, even flatulate! They have the sense of touch, but do they also have emotions? If plants truly did have feelings, would that mean they have a soul?

Astrophysicists say that the universe wraps around itself like a giant donut. If so, what was thought to be an infinite dimension is actually a torus, which means that we are literally stuck in a loop. Is a finite universe any indication of the existence of a multiverse? The universe is so fascinating because—even with all of the discoveries of modern science—it remains the greatest mystery of all time. The fact that we can never really know the actual shape and extent of the universe is the ultimate mindfuck.

If there were an irreversible portal that led to another dimension, would you go? If we only get one life here on Earth, would curiosity be enough for you to explore the unknown element of what could be a parallel universe? If we each had an assigned date of expiration, would you want to know yours? Could you choose between knowing the day, the month, or the year of your demise? Life seems to be the universe's thought experiment. Maybe we're simultaneously dead and alive like Schrödinger's cat.

Why is life so short? Time seems to move faster with each passing day, so it's hard to fully grasp how much time we may have left. I wonder why the human body is only built to last until around the century mark. If you could, would you want to live forever? To me, immortality would be a curse. To live is to suffer and watch others suffer despite the good times that you may have. All good things must come to an end. As life is a blessing, so is the mercy of death.

Life is a continuous thought experiment. Everyone has a different philosophy and the skepticism to challenge other philosophies. There's an enduring myth that we only use 10% of our brains. Despite this untruth, there's a boundless expanse in our minds for epistemic discovery. The mind is an ellipsis of infinite thought.

**FABIAN M.C. KUYKENDALL**

## *Theories of Conspiracy: Man-Made Facts & Fiction*

Conspiracism has become a global phenomenon. Due to social media influence on platforms like Twitter (X), Facebook, and YouTube, conspiracy theorists are ubiquitous. They describe themselves as truth-seekers, even though they create their own truths. They seem to exist just to oppose the consensus. These pseudo-rebels thrive on spreading fear through their own dissidence. It's unbelievable how other people fall for their theories without any factual evidence. The conspiracist motto seems to be, "You're not intelligent unless you question every aspect of reality."

Some people have a compulsive need to be extreme and radical in everything that they do and say. They convince themselves that everything is a conspiracy to make themselves feel like they know something that no one else knows—like they've "figured it out." Most conspiracy theorists don't accept facts, so they're not completely in touch with reality. They claim to be freethinking, but they really aren't open-minded at all. They're right and everyone else is wrong.

Conspiracy theorists spend far too much time over-thinking and over-analyzing. They're like bounty hunters, obsessively searching to uncover untruths. Their narcissism keeps them eager to enlighten the world about their game-changing revelations. They tend to have a paranoid, schizotypal view of the world. This delusional pathology causes them to create ridiculous belief systems of alternative facts. While some conspiracists give thought-provoking insight, it's hard to tell if most are revolutionaries or lunatics.

Many conspiracy theorists believe that the Moon landing was a staged Hollywood production. They also believe that Area 51 is home to extraterrestrial activity conducted by the government. These same people likely believe that climate change isn't real. I'll never understand why some people believe that Earth is flat. If that were so, why hasn't anyone ever reached the edge of Earth? What would that even look like? Would the seas just spill into an infinite abyss? Why don't people recognize that it's just not possible? Insanity is the outright refusal to accept proven facts.

Conspiracy theorists believe that the 9/11 attacks were an inside job. They believe that the twin towers collapsed by way of controlled demolitions. When the coronavirus became a worldwide pandemic, conspiracists purported that there was a link between the virus and 5G mobile networks. They believed that the virus was engineered by Big Pharma and the government for financial gain and used as a bioweapon for population control. They also believed that the Covid vaccine was used for mind control and sterilization. Meanwhile, hundreds of thousands of people were needlessly infected with the virus due to misinformation, and just as many lives were lost.

Holocaust denial is an antisemitic conspiracy theory dreamt up by historical revisionists who insist that the Holocaust was a hoax. There's an international Jewish conspiracy theory which claims that Jewish people are reptilian shapeshifters who are conspiring to take over the world. Those who concocted and/or believe this theory are clearly motivated by hate and prejudice. Many of the same conspiracists also believe in the so-called great replacement theory or "White genocide." They're convinced that abortion, immigration, and racial integration is all an effort to turn White people into a minority. This ridiculous theory is undoubtedly a result of their fear of losing White supremacy.

Conspiracy theories dominate right-wing politics. Conservatives reflexively assign conspiracy theories to any group of people they hate. The QAnon cabal is known for inventing these falsehoods to make it seem like they're "fighting the good fight" against what they allege to be a left-wing deep state of child molesters and Satan worshipers. They contend that mass shootings are staged and that the victims are portrayed by "crisis actors." This is an effort to shift blame so that they don't have to feel guilt or sympathy and can, instead, vilify the victims as part of their agenda to invalidate the need for gun control. Conservatives have a misinformation pathology that is utterly sickening.

The New World Order is an enduring conspiracy theory about the existence of a covert group of powerful figures who are plotting global domination. Today's Millennial/Zoomer generation know of the New World Order through the Illuminati. The Illuminati isn't a conspiracy theory as much as it is a countercultural obsession. Illuminati conspirophiles are consumed with symbolism and semiotics. Anytime they see entertainment media with pyramids or the illuminated "all-seeing eye," they assume that it portends a demonic, autocratic connection.

I believe that many conspiracy theories have a ring of truth. Throughout the ages, there have been more than enough reasons to believe in government cover-ups, assassination involvements, drug and weapon planting, espionage, etc. I understand why people have conspiracy theories since it goes against our nature as humans to trust. It's a shame that we have to be so hesitant and that we can't trust facts with confidence anymore. They say that if you don't stand for something, you'll fall for anything. I agree. However, I also think that if you take a stand for everything, it ultimately means nothing. Misinformation is dangerous, be careful whom you trust with the truth.

## *Intellectual Property: Can Originality Still Exist?*

Has everything already been said and done? Do our presumably ingenious epiphanies break new ground or just repeat the same cycle? History, indeed, repeats itself. Styles and trends are cyclical, recurring with every new generation. Part of the problem is, everyone has fair use of everything that's in the public domain. With all of the ground that's already been covered, there seems to be no untouched land left to discover on Earth.

I think that most people are just too lazy to be original. It's easier to replicate than it is to innovate. People would rather stick with what works than to take a chance. At this point, originality doesn't seem to be as important as profitability. Most of society feels an obligation of uniformity; therefore, they just conform to the status quo. There's so much competition when it comes to styles and ideas, so people resort to stealing other people's intellectual properties and claiming them as their own.

They say that imitation is the sincerest form of flattery. The thing is, everyone seems to think that they're being original when they "interpret" or give their version of a style or idea that's already been utilized many times before. People love to "pay homage" or be "inspired" by someone else's work because it frees them from the effort of coming up with something fresh. This mimicry isn't flattering at all, it's insulting. Besides, where's the artistic integrity in plagiarizing and making bootleg reproductions?

Reboots of old TV shows have an overrated popularity. For some reason, people think that it's a good idea to reheat stale french fries. No one seems to be utilizing their creative license to come up with something unique and progressive. With film remakes and music covers, people simply copy someone else's work and present it as new. This practice is highly reductive and pointless as it seldom adds anything worthwhile to the work. There's no wonder why lawsuits for copyright infringement are commonplace.

In the music industry, artists seem to follow musical templates. When composing music, there are only so many notes with which to work, so, inevitably, many songs end up sounding very similar. Also, with songwriters recycling the same clichéd themes of love, sex, and breakups, nothing in today's music sounds the least bit original. Is the industry severely limited, or are artists and producers just not trying hard enough?

Fashion and personal style rarely represent individuality. Today, it's more of a community property. People would rather buy into brands and be told what to wear and how to look based on what's en vogue. Effectively, we end up with everyone in the same mass-produced one-size-fits-all fashion. When people look and dress the same, they're likely seen as *being* the same. Why would one want to brand themselves that way?

Is there anything left to discover? Is there anything that has yet to be created? Since people don't seem to use imagination anymore, are there any new ideas left? Is time stuck in a perpetual reset? Are we just reliving what was already done eons ago? We seem to be stuck inside the box when it comes to ideas, trapped in a perpetual cycle of reruns and déjà vu. If there's nothing new remaining, what does that mean for future generations of humanity?

Since necessity is the mother of invention, there will always be new inventions. Technology demands that which is newer, bigger, faster, stronger, and better. Inventors are able to patent and trademark their work, but how much is an intellectual property really worth? You can't put a price on innovation because it inevitably leads to countless copycats. Nevertheless, because styles and trends are cyclical, we have to break the cycle by breaking new ground.

# CHAPTER 6 - SEX & SEXUALITY

### *Selling Sex: The Business of Bodies*

As they say, sex sells. Many companies use it shamelessly to market themselves, others hide it in their advertisements through subliminal messages—they even snuck the word *sex* into a scene from the children's movie *The Lion King*. Sex is such a powerful addiction that it's used to engage people subconsciously and entrance them into spending money. Such subliminal stimuli has proved to be effective psychological manipulation. Since sex sells, people sell it!

Sex in media is often filtered by censorship. Even with our culture being more progressive than it's ever been—and with so much worse content on TV and in real life—we still prioritize the restriction of sexual imagery. Television networks show actual murder scenes on true crime shows, but sex is somehow considered too explicit. Stopping short of pornography, I don't see anything severely damaging about showing sex scenes on basic TV at appropriate times. Generally speaking, however, our society is quite prudish, and sex is still taboo.

Pornography is much more widespread than it was a few decades ago thanks in large part to X-rated websites and streaming apps. Unfortunately, this gives children much easier access to pornographic imagery than they once had. It's quite unsettling to think of how common it is for kids to watch such explicit material. Porn gives people—especially young men—unrealistic expectations of what sexual experiences should be. The popular porn themes of today—which include violence, nonconsensual sex, and misogynistic sexism—set a dangerous precedent for sex education.

Prostitution has been called the world's oldest profession. Today, women unabashedly use their vaginas as credit cards. Adult entertainment is a multibillion-dollar industry. Along with pornography, it offers sex tourism, strip clubs, sex shops, erotic massage, etc. Even though it's completely natural to explore our bodies through self-manipulation, masturbation is somehow still seen as socially unmentionable. However, sex toys such as vibrators, dildos, and pocket pussies are extremely popular and a highly profitable sector of the adult entertainment industry.

Women have long been subjected to sexual objectification by men. "Breastaurant" chain *Hooters* is famous for its scantily clad waitresses who are made to advertise their physical assets in exchange for financial ones. Attempts at similar exploitation of men—like the short-lived *Hooters* counterpart *Tallywackers*—aren't nearly as profitable. Men are more willing than women to pay for a sexy/sexual experience, that's why they have the upper hand. Unfortunately, that financial power leaves women at the mercy of objectification.

"Pussy power" has given a new name and meaning to the feminist movement as more and more women find power in sexualizing their identity, but why is sex so often their path of liberation? Why do so many women use feminism as an excuse to objectify themselves? It's so much easier for them to sexualize their image than it is to intellectualize it. I do appreciate a progressive, sexually empowered woman, but it's a shame that a generation of young women have transformed themselves into plastic, mechanical thot-bots just to stay on trend.

Unfortunately, many of today's women attempt to justify "thot" culture by placing it under the guise of feminism. Everything about their so-called empowerment—from their wardrobe to their societal platform—revolves around sex. Often the self-appointed victims of "slut-shaming," they wish to be respected for their minds when all they show are their bodies. When you shamelessly use your body/sex to promote and support yourself, you can't blame people for thinking that's all that you are.

What's most troubling is the sexualizing of young girls by grown women. From pageant moms to dance moms, they paint these little girls in make-up that makes them look like 20-somethings, and they dress them in costumes that are disturbingly similar to what you'd see in strip clubs. As these women post pictures on image-sharing websites to show off their little girl's looks, they act as pushers for pedophiles, dealing them a free supply of inappropriate, underage imagery.

There was a time when "Lolita" themes in entertainment were common, even acceptable. Middle-aged men openly lusted after barely-pubescent "jailbait." The schoolgirl fantasy/fetish exploded in the '90s, perhaps most notably after the release of Britney Spears' "...Baby One More Time" music video. It's alarming to think of how pedophilia was so public, yet somewhat overlooked. We've definitely come a long way since then, thankfully.

What do we want more, money or sex? Sex or love? Sex and money seem to be an equally-desired co-op. People desire sex so much that they spend money, and people desire money so much that they sell sex. Sex and love are both powerful, but love is far more meaningful. Then again, sex and love go hand in hand because everyone loves sex.

A lot of people are health conscious and overly concerned with what they put into their bodies, but I'm just as concerned with what I put my body into. Sex is amazing, but promiscuity is dangerous, so it's good to be selective. I don't understand why so many people are opposed to using protection. Some people would rather wear a face mask against Covid than to wear a condom against STIs. Safe sex is still SEX! The safest sex is self sex. As long as you have a body, you're in business.

**FABIAN M.C. KUYKENDALL**

## *Ambiguous Species: Modern Gender Association & Identity*

Traditional gender roles are a thing of the past. Today's women are strong, independent bosses. Many women choose not to have children and, instead, focus on their careers. Many of today's men are sensitive, compassionate empaths who don't mind following the lead of a woman. More and more men are stay at home dads while the woman is the sole breadwinner. Men also put a lot more effort into their looks than they used to. Now, it's common for men to spend lots of money pampering themselves like women do.

We're all literally half man, half woman, yet, somehow, we're expected to possess only masculine or feminine traits. Women are expected to be obsessed with fashion and their appearance, especially to attract men. Men are expected to be obsessed with sports, cars, and beer, and to have a generally misogynistic attitude. Men are typically raised to be devoid of emotion and to exhibit a brutish machismo, toxic masculinity is encouraged. They are taught not to cry or be vulnerable, which would risk them being seen as feminine or weak. Essentially, men are expected not to be human.

In the industry of fashion modeling, why are the men called "male" models? They don't model other *men*, and the women aren't referred to as "female" models. It seems like society feels that it's necessary to mention a man's gender when he's a model because it doesn't fit into gender clichés. A lot of today's women appropriate the opposite gender in order to avoid these clichés, some even seem to have penis envy. They call themselves kings instead of queens, they reference their "balls" or their "dicks," and they basically go out of their way to project a masculine attitude. I don't know if this is just overcompensation in order to be seen as one of the guys or some form of extremist feminism.

In this new millennial age, conventional gender roles have been rearranged, while gender itself is becoming more and more androgynous. Some organizations have tried to eliminate gender altogether. MTV's Video Music Awards replaced its Best Male Video and Best Female Video categories with the all-gender-inclusive Artist of the Year. While inclusiveness is a great thing for society, is it really necessary to get rid of an identity in order to acknowledge another? Does someone have to completely disregard who they are in order to show acceptance to someone else?

I feel like our society is trying to mesh everyone together into a unisex gender—even the Mr. Potato Head toy has gone gender neutral. It's almost like we don't want to allow people to be male or female anymore. I think that this idea goes way too far—to the point of trying to force natural-born men and women to feel guilty for being who they are. I don't think that this is necessary for the sake of inclusion. It's more than possible for all of us to accept each other while continuing to be ourselves.

A species that began with male and female is gradually becoming one of numerous alternative genders. While I understand that many people grow up feeling like they were born as the wrong gender, I think it's unnatural for people to completely customize their own unique gender. Society is even trying to make the use of gender pronouns an obligation. Why is it so necessary to let everyone know if you identify as he/him, she/her, or they/them—unless you're non-binary? Soon, our sexual orientation will become mandatory public information as well.

Because of advancements in gender reassignment surgery, it's getting harder to determine a person's gender. Many transgender people—especially transgender women—withhold their biological origin from their partners, which—in many cases—has proved to be dangerous, even deadly. Some people have argued that transgender people should be obligated to disclose information regarding their sexual identity to their partners. There has also been much conversation about trans women choosing to identify simply as women. I truly empathize with those who feel like they were born as the wrong gender. However, you can't choose your gender just like you can't choose your sexuality, family, or race—which also means that you can't *change* your gender. I know that it's harsh and unfair, but such is life.

Many of today's youth struggle with gender dysphoria, and many parents offer gender-affirming treatment as an option for their children. However, I don't agree with this. As much as I believe that these parents love their children and would do anything to make them feel secure with who they are, I think that providing gender reassignment for children is irresponsible. Some children may feel like they are misidentified in their gender, but they're not mentally and emotionally capable of making the decision to irreversibly alter themselves. We talk a lot about the age of consent in regards to sexual intercourse, but doesn't that also apply to surgical procedures for gender affirmation?

In 2016, there was much debate about which public restrooms transgender people should use. Many people strongly felt that transgender people should use the restroom that represents the gender with which they were born. Most seemed to be concerned with the safety of children in these restrooms, citing the potential for sexual assaults. Personally, I think a good—if not obvious—alternative would be to add a third gender non-specific option. In a decision that was obviously based on fear and intolerance, Donald Trump banned transgender people from the military. There is absolutely no problem that this decision solves and, therefore, no reason for it. A person's transgender orientation is in no way an impairment that hinders their ability to serve their country.

There's also an ongoing debate about transgender athletes competing in gender-specific sports. While it's easy to argue that a transgender female has an unfair biological advantage and, therefore, shouldn't be allowed to compete with athletes who were assigned female at birth, they still shouldn't be discriminated against simply for being transgender. I'm not sure what the best solution is, but I don't think that any sport is going to categorize transgender athletes separately for the sake of fairness. Still, it is our obligation as a society to make room for everyone.

Unfortunately—in our American culture—we exaggerate and exploit any perceived form of oppression for our own selfish benefit. This mindset has turned many in the LGBTQ community into privileged victims. Many gay White people—mainly men—like to equate their homosexuality with Blackness. This allows them to attach their struggle to Black people in a way that authenticates it while trivializing ours. It seems like the more gains that are made for their community, the more they flex their victimhood. It's gotten to the point where if you simply disagree with their beliefs—even if you don't launch hateful protests or condemn them to hell—you're labeled as homophobic. Also, if you're not overly accommodating, the assumption is that you're homophobic.

The LGBTQ community understands the feeling of judgment, but they can be just as judgmental when it comes to straight people. Some of them even use their homosexuality as license to harass and verbally abuse those in the straight community with self-righteous hypocrisy. I understand the human nature of repeating what was done to you, but two wrongs never make a right. At the risk of sounding controversial, I have to say that the whole LGBTQ culture—at times—feels like it's being forced upon the mainstream. As more of the straight community embraces the LGBTQ community, it almost seems like we're expected—in some way—to convert to their sexuality. Our acceptance of them—even with their in-your-face tactics and protests—doesn't seem to be enough.

On *Celebrity Big Brother UK*, R&B singer Ginuwine rejected the advances of a transgender woman who attempted to kiss him. Ridiculously enough, this caused quite a stir on social media with people making accusations of "transphobia." Now, if the roles were reversed and Ginuwine forced his sexual advances on this transgender woman who did not want to kiss him, absolutely no one would make any claims of "heterophobia." In fact, I'm pretty sure that they would call it exactly what it is: sexual harassment. Everyone is entitled to their own sexual preference, and heterosexual individuals shouldn't have to kiss, have sex, or change their sexual identity in order to accommodate the LGBTQ community.

I've noticed the gradual feminization of straight and "metrosexual" men. From fashion—men in women's blouses and skirts—to media, the culture seems to be stripping men of their masculinity in order to put them more in line with an LGBTQ level of ambiguity. The idea is gender nonconformity, but so-called straight men look more than a little ridiculous carrying clutch purses. I think that too many of these men just want to partake in what they probably see as circus-like pageantry, but the point I'd like to make is that if you choose not to conform to gender norms, do so with purpose, not pageantry.

Commercial ads for certain medications seem to feminize illness. They sell the idea that headaches and depression are things that only women deal with. I understand that women are their target audience for many reasons—mostly financial—but I think that more men would feel comfortable buying these products if there wasn't such a stigma attached. As men, we commonly hide our gender insecurity behind the mask of masculinity. Although most of us are either too self-conscious or too proud to admit it, we want gender inclusivity just as much as women do.

The 2016 Chicago Cubs—as a means of celebration—traded fist bumps and chest bumps for cup bumps in which they press their groins against each other, which looks awkward and ridiculous. Given the hyper-macho world of sports and its overall negative attitude toward homosexuality, I find it to be ironic—even hypocritical—for these men to display such homo-erotic behavior. The sports world seems to say that it's a customary rite of passage to partake in these types of celebrations, but if you enjoy them too much, you're gay, and being gay is wrong. Needless to say, this sends not only the wrong message, but also a confusing mixed message.

On the MTV show *True Life,* there was an episode in which straight men performed sex acts with other men while filming pornography. The question is, can someone really be "gay for pay?" Is sexuality interchangeable? Recently, there has been much talk about sexual fluidity. Many people are choosing to forgo any specific sexual categorization and just be with whomever they're attracted to—regardless of gender—for as long as that attraction lasts. It makes sense why people are sexually fluid because—when you think about it—sexuality isn't just black or white, there's a gray area in between. Sexuality isn't just with whom you have sex. If a straight man or woman sees themselves as attractive, it stands to reason that they would also be attracted to someone of the same sex with similar characteristics.

I don't believe that sexuality is a choice, the choice is the way in which we act on it. What's odd is that most of us choose to make other people's sexuality our concern. A lot of people are against queer sexuality because of a learned prejudice, but it all boils down to the fact that they don't understand it. Some people are asexual, and that should be okay, but others feel obligated to judge and harass them simply for lacking sexual desire. Members of the LGBTQ community snub them because—ironically enough—they don't understand them. I'll never understand why people care so much about another person's sexuality. Who someone else fucks doesn't make *you* cum.

Some people who oppose the LGBTQ lifestyle also believe in gay conversion therapy. They feel that this lifestyle is a disease that can be treated or a demonic possession that can be exorcized. They use the Bible to preach that sodomy is unnatural. Some queer people even become victims of "corrective rape." What's really heartbreaking is that so many families disown their children or relatives simply for being gay. The Black community has a very conservative view of sexuality. Every Black woman has a gay male friend, but they'd be damned if their son were gay. Too many Black people see homosexuality as a defect from which they want to disassociate themselves. It's sad for me to see us be so intolerant and condemning of our own family, especially when the world has already rejected and condemned us for being Black.

In the case of homophobia, I don't think that "phobia" is the proper term to use; it's more about intolerance and ignorance. Therefore, one who is against homosexuality shouldn't be seen as homophobic, but, instead, homo-intolerant. Besides, a homophobe isn't afraid of homosexuals, they're afraid of homosexuality. They can't tolerate homosexuals because they fear that doing so might make them appear to be gay. They're insecure with their own sexuality because they actually might be gay. Homosexuality is seen as a weakness in men. People love to exploit this perceived weakness by questioning a man's sexuality. Everyone sees power in being normal and being a part of the majority. It's a mob mentality that makes us condemn those who are on the outside.

In an effort to counter the modern-day LGBTQ movement, many heterosexual men have organized a "straight pride" movement. While there shouldn't be an issue with anyone wanting to celebrate their culture or sexual orientation, you can't help but question the motive behind something like this. We live in a nation that despises when any group whose views differ from our own is at the center of national attention. Somehow, it makes us feel like we're not in power, an insecurity that demands that we rain on their parade. The difference between gay pride and straight pride, however, is that gay pride celebrates the right to exist without being bullied, discriminated against, beaten, or killed simply for being who you are; whereas straight pride seems more like a privileged majority's desperate cry for attention and a slap in the face to equality.

In June 2016, Omar Mateen shot and killed 49 patrons—injuring 53—at Pulse gay nightclub in Orlando. He was eventually killed in a shootout with police. What a pathetic waste of life. The fact that a man could hate homosexuality more than he valued his own life—or the lives of his wife and son—is just sad beyond description. Similarly, in November 2022, Anderson Lee Aldrich shot and killed 5 patrons at Club Q in Colorado Springs. This was yet another act of prejudice-motivated violence in an ever-growing list of mass shootings. I can't even attempt to wrap my head around the reason why a person would be driven to kill someone because of their sexuality, especially when it doesn't even affect *them*. I can't believe how dangerous it is to live as you are when your sexuality differs from what's "normal." I can't believe that we've normalized hate crimes.

In 2023, Tennessee issued a ban on public drag performance. In 2022, Florida passed its "Don't Say Gay" law to spite the LGBTQ community. The state's Conservative clan seems to think that classroom instruction about sexual orientation and gender identity will make their kids gay. The south has a way of silencing educators and preventing them from teaching things that they don't agree with or things that they don't want their kids to know about (slavery). What these selfish, prejudiced, irresponsible parents don't seem to realize is that homosexuality will always exist, and their children will inevitably know about it. No matter what you do, you can't prevent your child from being gay.

There are a prism of colors in the gay spectrum, a reflection of the diversity in the world. The LGBTQ initialism seems to be gaining almost every letter in the alphabet. I look forward to the day when sexuality and gender association don't matter. Being who you are and living as you wish to live should not be contingent upon tradition. No matter how you identify, you are here for a reason, and there's room for us all.

## *Age of Accountability: The Exposure of Rape Culture in America*

There has been an unspoken rape culture within college campuses for decades. There was a story involving a group of sexually frustrated frat boys who wanted to legalize rape, just an example of the delusional level of entitlement possessed by too many young men. Sexual assaults are frequently enacted by members of fraternities. They're known to engage in gang rape and "party rape" of drugged or intoxicated victims. These assaults often go unreported due to the victim being ashamed or fearful that no one will believe their story. Sexual aggression and rape tolerant attitudes make it easy for these men to feel like rape is justifiable. Fraternal clubs of alcohol, debauchery, and toxic masculinity are the perfect storm for rape culture.

As evidenced by general male culture, we simply don't know how to control our sexual urges, so we turn them into games wherein we fondle each other, which normalizes sexual harassment and sexual assault. It's an issue that desperately wants to progress to the point where everyone's body is community property and literally up for grabs. The topic of this bi-curious behavior can easily venture toward gay rape, which is still very taboo. This taboo—which involves fear, embarrassment, and manipulation—paralyzes men from speaking out against it. In many cases, if a man feels uncomfortable partaking in homo-erotic activity, he could very likely be ostracized and bullied by his peers for "acting like a bitch." Understandably, I'm sure that many guys—while yet uncomfortable—still play along out of fear and give in to what is ultimately abuse.

Rape culture controls much of the corporate world with sexism in the form of blackmail, bribes, tit for tat, and an all-around uncomfortable workplace environment for women. Since men are almost always in charge—and money trumps everything—their acts of sexual harassment easily go "unnoticed." Any male CEO who can bring in millions of dollars from corporate sponsors has free reign to do absolutely whatever he wants while his crimes are swept under the rug. This is the very reason why it took decades for Roger Ailes and Bill O'Reilly to finally be held accountable for their actions.

The most alarming issue here is that sexual assault has, indeed, become a culture. This culture is perpetuated and enabled by a "Boys will be boys" society that makes excuses for sexist rapists. Through victim shaming and victim blaming—"She was asking for it," "Look at the way she dresses"—they callously vilify the women who suffer the abuse. Rape culture has become normalized and exploited by men who feel an entitlement over a woman's body. They feel that it's okay to make sexual references and jokes toward their female colleagues or force inappropriate touching—even in the form of hugs—without the woman's consent.

This is an exercise of power which manifests itself through an utter and inexplicable lack of self-control. What these child-like men don't understand is that there are plenty of other alternatives to satisfy your carnal perversion, not everyone wants to be a part of your sexual experience. It's so pathetic to see the White male superiority complex be unable to grasp the fact that they're not entitled to touch, brush up against, or fondle women, no matter how the women dress or act. These men have a pathological belief that sexual gratification is owed to them by nature and that women provoke these violations. They follow the lead of their hero Donald Trump who says that it's okay to grab women "by the pussy."

Unfortunately, many working-class women feel like they have to put up with sexual mistreatment from male superiors in order to provide for their families. They're paralyzed with fear from the power that these men have over them—and these men are well aware of the fear that allows them to exploit this power—that's why so many women are willing to suffer this type of abuse for decades of their lives. This sad reality just becomes par for the course because they feel like there's nothing they can do to stop it and that they'll be worse off if they attempt to do so.

Rape culture is normalized in our minds from an early age, often through what we see on TV. The *Looney Tunes* character Pepé Le Pew is a cartoon skunk that makes constant aggressive advances toward a female cat named Penelope. He is narcissistic and only sees her rejections as flirtation; therefore, he is unable to take "no" for an answer. These images of harassment, stalking, and abuse are not the healthiest for a developing child. Pepé's character was removed from the 2021 film *Space Jam: A New Legacy*.

Rape culture also involves statutory rape—or unlawful sex with a minor—in which adults groom and sexually abuse underage individuals. Even if the sex is "consensual," adults take advantage of the fact that their victim cannot psychologically—or legally—consent to it. On the reality/crime TV show *To Catch a Predator*, men are caught at a sting house meeting (adult decoys posing as) minors for sex. These men—like countless others in America—prey upon underage teens in online chat rooms and social media, and manipulate them into sexual encounters.

Tragically, there's also a culture of rape that takes the form of pedophilia. In late 2017, former USA Gymnastics national team doctor Larry Nassar was convicted of sexually abusing over 200 girls and young women. This sick culture of child molestation is perpetuated by organizations like USA Gymnastics who enable and protect the abusers by ignoring the complaints of the abused. Many of the parents of these young athletes are also to blame for not trusting their children when they mention the abuse and for choosing to ignore the problem just because they don't want to cause another one.

Thanks to the changing tide of brave women speaking out, a growing list of renown men in power—including Harvey Weinstein, Leslie Moonves, Matt Lauer, Charlie Rose, R. Kelly, Russell Simmons, Sean Combs, Brett Ratner, Kevin Spacey, Michael Oreskes, and Al Franken—were finally brought to some form of justice for their sexual misconduct. The #MeToo movement continues to play a huge role in dismantling the system of sexual harassment and rape in America. In the age of accountability, rape culture will not prevail, and violators will be beholden to deserved punishment.

## *Punishment Paradox: The Pleasure of Pain*

Why is it that people find pleasure in pain? Those who partake in the BDSM lifestyle of bondage, discipline, dominance, submission, sadism, and masochism seem to be gluttons for punishment. They aren't just the typical leather-clad freaks who engage in dark erotica in underground sex dungeons; they're your everyday lawyers, bankers, and retail workers who enjoy master/slave role play and humiliation involving urination and defecation. This seems like psychosexual perversion on the outside, but what's underneath it?

The book and movie series *Fifty Shades of Grey* became an obsession for millions of women. A lot of bored, lonely, sexually unfulfilled housewives and horny young professionals found this story very appealing. The idea of the handsome billionaire who shows his desires for a woman through acts of sexual violence seemed to be their perfect love story. So many women feel love through toxicity in relationships. It's disturbing how much they normalize it through social media content and movies like *Grey*.

Many women say that they feel sexually empowered by BDSM relationships, but how does a woman gain empowerment by submitting herself to a man? Doesn't a man's desire for dominance over a woman reveal his weakness instead? When a man enacts these fantasies in the dominant role over a woman, is it sex or sexism? At what point does role-playing become domestic abuse? The whole submissive, masochistic realm seems to appeal to women with low self-esteem who don't care much about themselves or their well-being.

Is the propensity for BDSM activity indicative of animal nature or a mental defect? It's unnatural for someone to be sexually aroused by inflicting pain and torment on someone else. Enacting rape fantasies, choking, pulling hair, slapping, piercing, and genital torture are red flags of sexual sadism disorder. To fetishize dangerous, life-threatening behavior is abnormal and antithetical to sexual pleasure, so why do so many people find pleasure in these paraphilic activities? Why do moans of pleasure and moans of pain sound virtually the same?

Are those who engage in BDSM activity more liberated than those who don't? Are they boldly living in their truth and, therefore, less likely to have mental health issues? Many of us have involved whips, chains, blindfolds, and handcuffs in our sex lives, but it starts to become extreme when we introduce ball gags, leashes, and nipple clamps to the routine. For doms and sadists, it's obviously about exerting power over their partners, but—on a universal level—maybe the pain makes it easier for us to appreciate the pleasure.

# CHAPTER 7 - MEDIA & ENTERTAINMENT

***Who Killed R&B?: The Reductive State of Contemporary Music***

The line that once separated rap from rhythm & blues has unfortunately been blurred. The two genres have been meshed together not only by artists, but by consumers and critics who can't distinguish their differences. These people—having no idea of what R&B actually is—often use the term in reference to anything that's considered to be Black music. If an artist sings and they have even the slightest "urban" edge, they're automatically categorized as R&B. Some of the confusion stems from a tired trend in which a lot of today's so-called R&B music is partially rapped and partially sung. It seems that every singer wants to rap, and every rapper wants to sing. However, melodic rapping does not equate to actual singing and hardly qualifies as real R&B.

Until recently, the musical landscape was a "trap" wasteland. Trap music dominated pop and urban radio. The majority of this music reflects and promotes not only a negative lifestyle, but also a negative mindset. Rap in particular has never had the best public perception—so much so that when the media tries to disparage an R&B singer like Chris Brown, they call him a "rapper." Most trap music is about worshiping money and belittling those who don't have it. It's about focusing all attention and energy on your haters, hoping to provoke their envy for your self-proclaimed greatness. It's about unabashed negativity, which perpetuates a negative culture. How can one deliberately surround themselves with so much negativity and still be happy? Music should—at the very least—make you feel good.

A problem with music—and art in general—is its over-fixation on dark emotions like sadness and anger. It's the reason why dramatic films win the Best Picture Oscar almost exclusively and why happiness—as it relates to music—isn't taken seriously as art. Artists seem to think that showing emotion only means expressing sadness. I don't think that people like to associate happiness with emotion because—to some degree—they fear it. Happiness doesn't seem to be real enough to define genuine emotion so—artistically and subconsciously—we rid ourselves of it.

We give so-called artists money and clout for songs that talk about how much money and clout they have. We hold them to an increasingly poor standard, giving them success for low-quality music, which enables them to be lazy and not earn their success. As it does with every generation, music has changed drastically. Songs are generally almost two minutes shorter than they used to be, and bridges were dropped from songs altogether. Trap music overall is severely lacking in artistry and imagination because too many rappers chase trends, and too many producers let technology dictate what they create. Generally speaking, we don't see music as an art form anymore. It seems to be a mere hobby for those who create it and a cheap morsel for those who consume it.

Many people have said that music-based social media platforms—namely TikTok—have ruined the music industry. These platforms allow music to be cheapened into petty gimmicks. Because of the easy access and exposure, there are more artists, songs, and microtrends than anyone can keep up with. The problem is, there are too many songs and not enough hits. There are too many artists and not enough stars. Another growing issue is the role of artificial intelligence in music. There are AI music generators and simulators that allow users to basically cheat their way to producing professional music. This technology also allows them to create deep fake songs by artist clones. The ability to mimic an artist's voice on a record puts the music industry in messy, disturbing territory.

It's ridiculously inaccurate how record sales are measured today. It doesn't make sense to equate a certain number of streams to an actual record sale. Because of streaming, no one really buys music or owns physical copies of music anymore. Music is virtually free. Before the streaming era, owning tangible records was an accomplishment that gave you an appreciation for the music. When you purchased an album of your favorite artist, there was an excitement—a thrilling anticipation for what you were about to hear. The way that you consumed the music was more of an experience than it is today. People actually listened to complete albums—not just random tracks—which painted the soundscapes of memorable moments in their lives.

The beauty of today's music industry is that everyone gets a chance, but the downside is that *everyone* gets a chance. The truth is, not everyone deserves a chance because not everyone possesses an adequate level of talent. Back in the '90s when the industry was less accessible and more selective, the quality of music was inarguably better than it is today. Every genre had elite representation on the charts and airwaves. Artists were properly developed by record companies, and, thereby, prepared for stardom when they made their debut. Unfortunately, there doesn't seem to be many—if any—true superstars among today's crop of artists.

Everyone who considers themselves an artist or an entertainer is constantly fighting for attention among their peers. They're desperate to be seen and heard because they feel like they have something worthwhile to say. The amount of attention they receive is critical in determining the amount of success they'll have. Many artists rely on TikTok microtrends to propel them to the top of the charts, which is yet another reason for the poor quality of music. Artists have even found ways to cheat their way to number-one records through merch packaging and deeply-discounted first-week prices. They've made music to be all about the "look" and the very short-lived moment.

Non-R&B artists who want to be associated with the genre constantly try to redefine it for their benefit. They use the R&B brand to make themselves seem edgy and unique when they're actually basic pop artists. All of this culture catfishing has created a whole new set of problems for R&B music. Some pop artists—like Justin Beiber—have no reservations about appropriating the R&B genre and flexing their privilege within it. Mainstream audiences are much more likely to buy R&B music when a pop artist performs it instead of a true R&B artist. Beiber himself has made thirsty efforts to be seen as an R&B artist, even demanding that his music be placed in the R&B Grammy categories.

There's a long, well-known history of White artists appropriating Black music, the most famous of which is Elvis Presley. Presley is regarded as "The king of rock 'n' roll" after "borrowing" music—and much of his style—from Black artists. The Beatles, The Rolling Stones, and many other White acts were inspired by—if not, outright stole from—Black artists like Chuck Berry and Little Richard, to whom they gave little to no credit. White supremacy in music allowed for the theft of Black music without repercussions. Today, that entitlement still exists. Rock and country music—while dominated by White musicians—is completely derivative of Black music like R&B, gospel, jazz, and blues, which has been taken over by White musicians as well.

What constitutes good music will always be subjective. Just about every year, there are "all-time" best songs, albums, and artists lists compiled by trend-chasing Millennials and Zoomers instead of actual music historians. Quality is constantly invalidated by a changing culture. It's truly sad to see music reduced to what it is today. I know that every generation complains about how things were much better in their younger days, so for me to say so now makes me feel ... like I'm right! It's time to bring R&B back. It's time to bring hip-hop back. It's time to bring rock back. It's time to bring music back!

### *And the Validation Goes To ...: The Overvaluation of Award Shows*

Entertainment award shows are marred by politics. They've always been suspected of being rigged, which is easy to believe since the nominees literally buy their awards—or, at least, their nominations. Politics in the selection process of these awards are like PEDs in sporting events: They discredit all merit and deny any sense of achievement that comes with winning. It's become apparent that these awards aren't given out based solely on artistic value.

The Grammys in particular lost the final straw of credibility for me when they completely snubbed The Weeknd for his album *After Hours*, which was widely considered to be the best album of 2020. They denied him of a single nomination allegedly because he chose to perform at the Super Bowl and not the Grammy telecast. The Recording Academy is ruled by executives and massive corporations whose sole motivation is money, which leads to corruption through abuses of power. They know exactly how badly music artists covet these awards and the career boost that can come with winning, so they dangle these trophies in front of them like carrots to a rabbit.

The Grammys have long been culturally clueless regarding the current musical landscape, especially when it comes to hip-hop. I still remember back in 2001 when Eminem's brilliant—and now classic—*The Marshall Mathers LP* lost to Steely Dan's *Two Against Nature* for Album of the Year. In fact, despite being the predominant genre in music for over two decades, only two hip-hop albums—*The Miseducation of Lauryn Hill* and *Speakerboxxx/The Love Below*—have won Album of the Year in the entire history of the Grammys, and those albums were heavily infused with soul/R&B and alternative/pop. If a White rapper of Eminem's caliber isn't good enough to win Album of the Year, then it's all too obvious that the Grammys just don't respect hip-hop as an art form.

At the 58th annual Grammy Awards in 2016, Taylor Swift became the first female to win Album of the Year twice as a lead artist, beating Kendrick Lamar's *To Pimp a Butterfly*. Swift's *1989* was the year's best-selling album and boasted many hit singles, while Lamar's album was the year's most critically-acclaimed.

It's been said that the Grammys tend to reward sales and popularity when it comes to the big four awards—Best New Artist, Album, Record, and Song of the Year—but in the year prior to Swift's win, Beck took home the top prize for his off-the-radar *Morning Phase* over Beyoncé's critical and commercial eponymous smash.

At the 59th annual Grammy Awards in 2017, Adele won Album, Record, and Song of the Year, and became the first person ever to win all three twice. In her acceptance speech for Album of the Year, she famously suggested that Beyoncé should have won, instead, for her "monumental" *Lemonade* album. *Lemonade* was—almost unanimously—the most critically-acclaimed album of the year and was the best-selling album globally in 2016. Upon winning for her album *25*, Adele seemed to feel a sense of guilt for an unfair privilege that was given to her. She seemed to be very aware of a biased system that allowed artists like her to win over artists who are just as—if not more—deserving.

At the 65th annual Grammy Awards in 2023, Beyoncé became the most decorated person in the show's history when she won her 32nd trophy. Even with so many wins, she was yet again overlooked for Album of the Year. Prior to the ceremony, there was an article in Variety magazine in which Grammy voters admitted to voting against Beyoncé in the major categories specifically because she'd already won so many awards. These voters admitted to giving biased votes to artists who weren't necessarily deserving, and they also admitted to not actually listening to every nominee in the given category, even though that's literally their job.

It's become clear that the Grammys favor artists whose music/race is more acceptable to the mainstream audience. Perhaps every decade or so, there's an exception to this idea when an artist of color is simply too dominant to be overlooked—like Michael in '84 or Whitney in '94. Although often nominated, artists of color are usually shut out of wins in the big four categories. Instead of gaining the prestige and legacy that comes with winning in these categories, they're relegated to the lesser genre-based categories as a means of apathetic consolation. At one point, the Grammys even had a Best

*Urban* Contemporary Album category, which might as well have been called Best Race Record.

A major part of this decades-long problem is that Grammy winners are decided by mostly older White men who vote instinctively—and almost exclusively—for other White people. Former Recording Academy president Deborah Dugan has even made claims of the Academy's corruption and favoritism. They tend to focus only on artists with the biggest sales and/or artists with a more "traditional," conservative sound. They've also been known to award artists posthumously just to make up for a lack of prior recognition. This all begs the question: Why isn't it possible to just award the *best* music?

Obviously, what's considered to be the best is highly subjective, but based on the Grammy's picks for Album of the Year for the past few decades, are we really supposed to believe that White people just make better music than everyone else? Maybe the voters think that this bias—or BS—goes unnoticed, but we see it year after year. They'll shower Black artists with dozens of nominations just to boost ratings by having them in attendance, but deny them any major award. Basically, Black music is good enough to entertain their viewers, but not good enough to win Album of the Year.

As a teenager, I used to fantasize about the thrill of winning a Grammy one day. As an adult, I've realized that all of the politics, bias, and corruption that goes into awarding these trophies makes them utterly meaningless. Besides, we live in a subjective world. There's no one, and no group of people, who can determine what is truly the *best*— especially when comparing apples to oranges—so why does almost every artist constantly seek Grammy validation? The Grammys have made it extremely evident that they don't respect Black people enough to give us fair consideration. Black people: In case you didn't know, we don't need their validation in order to be valid.

When the nominees for the 88th annual Academy Awards were announced, it was revealed that—for the second consecutive year—no Black actors received nods in any of the four acting categories. Due to this lack of diversity, the #OscarsSoWhite campaign was born, and celebrities like Jada Pinkett-Smith and Spike Lee decided to boycott the ceremony. This came after decades of racial oversights by the Motion Picture Academy.

At the 2002 Oscars ceremony, Halle Berry became the first—and as of 2023, the only—Black woman to win Best Actress for her performance in *Monster's Ball*. When Viola Davis won Best Supporting Actress in 2017 for *Fences*, she reportedly chose to submit her nomination for the supporting category even though she had a leading role. I guess history showed that she had pretty much no chance of winning otherwise.

As Black people, it seems like we're constantly seeking approval from White people to validate our accomplishments and our success. Hearing these stories of award show snubs every year really puts my life goals into perspective. I had to ask myself, why would winning something like an Academy Award be so important? What would that mean? It wouldn't make me better than anyone else, and it wouldn't be the sole justification of my success. That's not to say that we as Black people shouldn't aspire to win these type of awards if that's what we want, but we can't allow ourselves to be defined by them.

Granted, anyone who works hard at their craft would love to be acknowledged for it, and—for most people—the Academy Award is the epitome of entertainment excellence. However—as Black people—why aren't we as appreciative of awards that come from our own community, such as the NAACP Image Award and the BET Award? Why don't we hold these awards in that same regard? Many Black celebrities don't even show up in support of these awards shows, yet they lustily chase after the White-dominated awards that supposedly represent the elite.

Ultimately, The #OscarsSoWhite campaign did help to spark some changes for diversity, including a revamp of the mostly-White voting board in favor of more representation from people of color. Unfortunately, I can't help but wonder if future Black nominees will be chosen based on their merit or just for the sake of inclusion. Are we really at a point where affirmative action must be implemented at awards shows?

Awards are just awards. They're tangible representations of an achievement, not the achievement itself. Winning at an awards show mainly provides a moment to be at the center of a large telecast and to be celebrated with the adulation of your peers. After the award is won, the moment is over, so the award begins to depreciate in value. Awards don't make you—or your life—any better.

**FABIAN M.C. KUYKENDALL**

## *Virtual Reality: The Scripted Manipulation of Life*

Reality television is the junk food of entertainment. It has no substance or nutritional value. Every so-called reality show is scripted, manufactured, and manipulated. Reality isn't even real anymore. People don't want to be real, they just want to be seen. It seems like everyone is filming every second of their lives through the lens of their smartphones, turning mind-numbing minutia into social media content. Somehow, life has become a reality show.

Producers of reality television that appeals to the "urban" and LGBTQ demographics seem to abide by a specific formula for success: Cast a group of attractive, little-known, moderately successful fame whores, put them in a room together, and encourage them to fight. This formula has proved to be successful for shows like *Basketball Wives*, *Married to Medicine*, and *The Real Housewives* franchise.

It's fascinating to see a group of middle-aged women willingly embarrass themselves for entertainment. Most of the "real housewives" aren't actually wives at all, but they all share the commonality of shameless desperation. It's sad how comfortable they are with being man-made women who only have any bit of notoriety because they married or slept their way into it. They're determined to present and maintain an illusory image of wealth and importance to mask the fact that they're miserable.

For the sake of portraying this fake reality, everyone is trying to keep up with the Joneses or the Kardashians. The Kardashian clan is so obsessed with fame and attention, they don't want to live a second of their lives off camera. Everything about them—from their scripted reality show to their cosmetically manufactured body parts—reeks of fakeness. I still don't understand how they've managed to hypnotize millions of people into watching them do absolutely nothing. It's amazing how you can gain reality show superstardom by virtue of lying on your back—or stomach—for a sex tape.

Stars of the *Love & Hip-Hop* franchise go out of their way to prove themselves, desperately reaching for relevance. The producers pull the strings, and their puppets dance. They come up with fake storylines for staged scenes of trifling drama. They make the cast look like oblivious fools as they make money off of them. It's clear that these "reality stars" have no self-respect as they sell their souls for a reality *check*. Some even go as far as changing their sexuality just to have a storyline. Most of them live outside of their means, clinging hopelessly to delusions of stardom.

For decades, the cheap, trashy talk shows of Jerry Springer and Maury Povich have earned big ratings and endorsement dollars by exploiting ignorant (often Black) people—Jerry with his bell-ringing, fight-baiting fare, and Maury with his signature revelations of "You are ... *not* the father!" I'll never understand why so many people would want to go on national TV and make buffoons of themselves. It's cringe-inducing to see the over-directed, exaggerated reactions to DNA and lie detector test results. The producers seem to salivate at the chance to make a spectacle at the expense of their clueless guests. Even Jerry and Maury have relished in saying "baby daddy" at every chance.

True crime shows like *Dateline* and *20/20* turn real-life tragedies into shameless entertainment. These shows seem to feed people's obsession with death and murder. If people were, instead, obsessed with life and living, imagine how much better the world would be. Television is my emotional support device, so it's troubling to see such dark, depressing content taking over so many time slots. It feels like sitcoms and comedy are going extinct. No one wants to laugh anymore. All we want to see is crime, violence, and drama. It's sickening to know that this is the type of reality in which so many people choose to indulge.

News outlets—both national and local—seem more concerned with entertaining than informing. They sensationalize bad news with exclamatory exaggeration just for ratings, keeping society inundated with constant negativity. They manipulate stories for their own melodramatic excitement, scripting their own reality. They unabashedly turn reality into a circus at the expense of real people's misfortune.

Reality television bears no resemblance to real life. Real life isn't manipulated and contrived. You may think that the cameras enhance who you are, but who are you without the façade of fame and wealth? Who are you when the cameras are off? Society has a warped sense of reality. Reality needs a reality check.

**FABIAN M.C. KUYKENDALL**

## *In Technicolor: The Roles of Minorities in Film & Television*

In Hollywood, you're only marketable if you appeal to White audiences, and you're only relatable if White people like you. For minorities, this presents a constant challenge to not only seek acceptance from the mainstream, but to also be given the opportunities to play quality roles. When the film and TV industry offers roles to minorities—particularly Black people—they're very specific with which type they choose. Hollywood is a chronic offender of interchangeable colorism. They never see the issue with replacing a dark-skinned Black actor with a light-skinned, mixed-race one. While it's true that Black people are made in a variety of colors—all of which are beautiful—it's not okay for Hollywood to give favor to what they feel is the "good Black" while presenting a diverse, progressive façade.

For the movie *Straight Outta Compton*, there was an infamous casting call seeking "A-girls" who were "the hottest of the hottest" and of any ethnicity, and—on the opposite end—"D-girls" who were "poor, not in good shape" and specifically "African American" with a "medium-to-dark skin tone." The casting agent who posted this racist announcement—a White woman, Kristan Berona—issued the standard insincere apology for what I'm sure she sees as a typical Hollywood practice. The audacity and entitlement of these casting companies is indicative of the prevalence of racism, colorism, and sexism in the entertainment industry.

Some Black people argue that more films about slavery need to be made so as not to allow this country to forget such an important part of history. Judging by social media, however, this country is well aware of slavery with many racists posting that we should "bring back slavery." Motion pictures—although mostly fiction—have an immense power of persuasion that manipulates how we view each other as people. In what often feels like an agenda that's being pushed on the world, White people are continuously portrayed in films as superheroes, kings, and gods; whereas Black people are too often presented as—and, therefore, perceived as—slaves. It's extremely necessary for the world to know that that's not all we were, and that's definitely not what we are. It's important that we realize the implications of this issue.

Films about slavery feel very exploitative—especially in today's world—and I am very certain that we've seen enough. Constantly reminding the world that Black people were once slaves only reinforces the bigoted thinking of those who want to return us to slavery. These films offer little to nothing in the name of progress and positive change; although, sadly, they seem to be the only casting opportunities for many Black actors in film. Hollywood seems to think that this exploitation of Black people is okay because of the film's often "happy ending." Either way, the making of these films must stop. Slavery should not be a movie genre.

For some reason, a lot of White filmmakers feel the need to tell our story for us. That story always seems to be about us being victims of their racism, and the best way to depict that is, apparently, through slavery. I've yet to see or hear of a film in which they tell their own story as it relates to racism, why they're racist, and what they need to do to change.

Filmmaker Quentin Tarantino seems to have a weird obsession with Blaxploitation, which makes sense given his repeated exploitation of Black people. In his film *Django Unchained*, yet another slavery film, the word *nigger*—on which he seems to have a juvenile fixation—is said over 100 times. There's a typical White savior protagonist by the name of Dr. King Schultz—which is basically a White-washing of Dr. Martin Luther King Jr.—not to mention the lurid glorification of slavery and violence for entertainment. People like Tarantino get to live out their sick, racist fantasies under the guise of subjective art and are rewarded for it. *Django*'s "White savior," played by Christoph Waltz, and its mastermind screenwriter, Tarantino, both received Academy Awards for their work.

It's hard to comprehend why so many White men feel the need to give a stereotypical impression of what they think a Black man is. It's like they have a compulsive instinct that they simply don't have the will to resist. It's weird. They also do this to Mexicans, Indians, Chinese people, etc. In the film *Tropic Thunder*, Robert Downey Jr. was painted in blackface to portray a Black man—for which he was nominated for an Academy Award. Were there no qualified Black men to fill the role, or was this Hollywood's perfect excuse to put on a modern day minstrel show? For decades, White actors have voiced

Black and brown animated characters on shows like *The Cleveland Show* and *The Simpsons.* Only recently has Hollywood begun to rectify this racist exploitation.

Roles in film and television are often White-washed in order to "appeal to a wider audience." Even historical, biographical roles that depict the lives of celebrated people of color are rewritten to show the heroic protagonist in a *white* light. Almost every film about ancient Egypt is made up of White people cast in roles of royalty and nobility, which obviously should be portrayed by people of African descent. Somehow, Hollywood feels like it's okay to deny people of color their aristocratic history and force the world to believe that Ramesses II, Nefertiti, Akhenaten, and other African monarchs were White.

On the small screen, very few leading roles are afforded to Black people—and other people of color—beyond trashy reality shows. This simply mirrors what we've all come to expect in this society: The majority rules, and we're not comfortable enough to vary too much from that rule. The Hollywood script is almost always the same: A White male protagonist—who is much desired by all women—defeats the racially interchangeable antagonist, saves the world, and gets the woman. Even in cases of interracial relationships—which are becoming more frequent, but still seem a bit taboo—there's likely a White male alongside a defenseless woman of color.

Why are interracial couples more acceptable when they involve a White male? In film, TV, and especially advertising, it seems that about 90% of interracial couples consist of a White man with a woman of color. There's always an agenda when it comes to advertising, so the message that they're sending is very clear. It bothers me that—with all that has progressed in the 21$^{st}$ century—racial minorities are still mostly seen as ancillary characters. The film and television industry has the locked mindset of keeping White men in leadings roles, or roles of power.

For much of the 2010s, there was an effort to add more diversity to major network TV shows. We welcomed sitcoms like *Black-ish*, which features an all-Black cast, and *Fresh Off the Boat*, which features an all-Asian cast. These shows were a refreshing change of pace and really funny, high-quality programming. However, they were still seen by some people as a "Black show" and an "Asian show" instead of shows about the human condition interpreted by people who happen to be Black and Asian. The point is, diversity and inclusion on TV—in the form of groups of people whose culture we might not be familiar with—should not interfere with the fact that we all relate to one another.

Representation matters. How we're portrayed on the screen is essentially how we see ourselves and what we can or can't be. Therefore, it's up to us to control our own narratives. We can no longer allow people who don't know our story to tell it for us. We also can no longer wait for opportunities to be given to us. We have the power to create our own opportunities and change the way that we're seen through the lens of Hollywood.

# CHAPTER 8 - KNOWLEDGE & EDUCATION

*Erasure: The Miseducation of America's Youth*

Writers and publishers are attempting to rewrite history in today's school textbooks. In describing the Atlantic slave trade, they write that slaves were "immigrants" from Africa who came to America for "work." The problem is, slaves were kidnapped and stolen from their homeland, and—as slaves—they did slave labor, they didn't earn wages. It's beyond despicable that these writers/publishers would dare to sugarcoat and whitewash such a horrible crime against humanity. It's inexplicable how they promote their conservative viewpoints by means of racial erasure at the expense of the students' education. It is the writer's, publisher's, and the school faculty's professional and moral obligation to teach the unmitigated truth.

Southern states have passed bills to prevent teachers from discussing critical race theory in class—even though it isn't taught to K-12 students. They're doing everything in their power to make sure that children believe that slavery never existed and racism is just a figment of imagination. They can teach kids about wars that claimed the lives of countless people—because it makes White people look like patriotic heroes and martyrs—but God forbid that kids learn about slavery and make White people feel guilty or "uncomfortable." For them, denying slavery means denying the systemic racism that still persists today. However, the internet will always exist, and children will meet and befriend people of color throughout their lifetime. Therefore, political parents: Your children will inevitably find out about slavery and systemic racism, and they'll grow to resent you for keeping them in the dark by trying to hide the truth.

In July 2023, Florida approved a curriculum to teach middle school students the "personal benefits" of slavery. This curriculum insists that enslaved Black people learned valuable skills and trades by the grace of their enslavement. Many GOP bigots questioned whether Black people would have really been better off without slavery. The efforts that they make to sugarcoat the horrors of slavery are mind-blowing. I'm stunned by the audacity that they have to insult us—and our intelligence—with the notion that White people did us a favor by enslaving us.

Florida's "Grand Wizard" governor Ron DeSantis issued a state ban on an advanced-placement African American studies course for high school students in 2023, claiming that the course "lacks educational value." As part of his pathetic "Stop Woke" campaign, he's made it his life's mission to end all conversations about race and gender in public schools. He's determined to make his followers believe that diversity and inclusion is anti-White because it goes against White supremacy. He said, "we believe in education, not indoctrination," yet he manipulated ways for Florida to indoctrinate by omission. Florida has gone on a crusade to ban Black authors and Black literature in an effort to eliminate our history and our contributions to America. However—whether they want to believe it or not—what will never change is the fact that Black history is American history.

A diligent effort needs to be made to preserve Black history. One of the main problems that comes from White people teaching Black history to children—especially children of color—is that many of them only teach what *they* want them to know, which is almost always more about slavery instead of the countless accomplishments and innovations of Black people. What teachers—and all of America—need to learn is that Black History Month was not created to celebrate slavery, nor was it created to constantly remind people about slavery.

Every Black History Month, there are racist, ignorant teachers who make headlines for their unthinkable actions. In 2023, a Miami teacher made her preschool students wear Blackface. In 2018, a teacher from the Bronx conducted a revolting slave trade demonstration to her mostly-Black class. The teacher selected 3 Black students to lie on their stomachs on the floor of the classroom while she stood on their backs so that they could "see how it feels to be a slave." It's disturbing to think that these are the people who shape the minds of the future of our nation. It's disheartening to know that a teacher would want to diminish the self-esteem and self-worth of an entire race of students.

Many schools and classrooms in America today are still segregated. In August 2021, it was alleged that an Atlanta elementary school principal segregated students by race. The reason for this educational apartheid was, supposedly, to help Black students deal with feeling isolated in a predominately White school. Apparently, this principal didn't understand that separate accommodations are inherently unequal and unconstitutional. Many urban schools with predominantly Black and Hispanic students are under-funded and I believe that this is because these children aren't expected to amount to anything. It's a sad truth that students of color have to be among White students in order to receive the same educational privileges.

Black students are often put in special education classes after being misdiagnosed with a learning disability. Unfortunately, too many of these students accept this misdiagnosis and use it as an excuse to fail. These children usually suffer from ADD or ADHD and, therefore, have trouble keeping focus, which is often passed off as misbehavior. Instead of being given the proper attention, these children are punished for something that they can't control. A lot of times, the help that they receive is in the form of overmedication. They're prescribed harmful drugs that completely change their personality to make it easier for the teacher to control them. How can children be educated when they're turned into drugged-out zombies? Doctors and teachers: You have to do better, it's your job.

Many jaded teachers belittle and discourage their students from chasing their dreams. They revel in diminishing the self-esteem of innocent little minds all because life didn't work out as well for themselves as they'd hoped. Some teachers dissuade minority children from prestigious career paths just because they feel that the child's race doesn't fit the role. This is why it's so important that parents are their children's first teacher and that they continue to teach them what their teachers don't.

It bothers me to know that some teachers have underachieving students whom they can't get through to—or are too lazy or apathetic to continue trying—so they just give up on them. They end up passing these students to the next grade level with the rest of their class, but sometimes it's necessary for a child to be "left behind"—especially if they are not prepared well enough to advance. I believe that it does a child a disservice to pass them on just to get rid of them and make them someone else's problem. How does that help them? They need to learn, and it is a teacher's duty to adequately teach them what they need to learn before moving them along.

Many children—in lieu of education—are forced into child labor. It's such a shame how negligent, heartless adults strip children of their future by forcing them to work for their own selfish benefit. These children not only miss out on their education, they miss out on their childhood. They're essentially forced into slavery, working in fields and sweatshops to profit able-bodied adults. Poverty and lack of schools will never be a good enough reason to exploit children. They shouldn't have to deal with adult issues. If children are our future, we should be preparing them for *their* future by educating them, not forcing them to support us.

As parents and as adults, we have to be responsible with what we teach our children. Their education should never be intended to gain an advantage for ourselves. We can't keep using them as pawns to serve our agenda. As education is being stifled by revisionist political campaigns, it's more important than ever that we learn America's true history. The problem with history, however, is that it's always told from someone else's perspective, so we can never really know the whole truth.

## *Idiotic Intellect: Dumbing Down Society*

The difference between wise and dumb is wisdom. People say that we're getting dumber as a society. It seems like the more that this is said, the more that people try (unsuccessfully) to prove that they're the exception; others simply don't care. These days, it's not about how smart you are; it's about how smart people *think* you are. You can talk a good game, but—when it comes down to it—are you smarter than a 5$^{th}$ grader?

It's annoying when people say certain words or phrases in order to sound intelligent, especially when they fail to use these words or phrases correctly. *Ironic* is one of the most criminally misused words. The same can be said for *literally* as both words are too often used to explain the exact opposite of the intended statement—like when people say that they *could* care less when they actually couldn't. Use of the word *invaluable* is about as needless and pretentious as it gets, especially since it means the exact same as the word *valuable*. Also, the phrase "for all intents and purposes" is often mistakenly replaced with "for all intensive purposes," which makes no sense at all. These catachreses just highlight our collective stupidity.

What's really ridiculous is when well-known and respected dictionary publications promote the dumbing down of the English language by accepting acronymic slang like *BFF* and *MILF*, and abbreviated drivel like *whatevs* and *cray*. It seems like there are hundreds of nonsensical neologisms added to the lexicon every year. I can't believe that we continue to turn such idiotic idiolect into an actual language. Everyone's mental capacity is customized, but the dunce cap is one-size-fits-all.

Everyday technology has adults communicating like 12-year-olds. First, we eliminated the need for vocal conversation with the advent of texting. Now, we've replaced text with emojis. The de-evolution of speech is painfully apparent with Gen Z. It went from "I can't even deal with this right now" in the '90s to "I can't even deal" to "I can't even" to simply "I can't." That pretty much sums it up: They can't. What they can't seem to do is exert enough energy to finish a sentence. Ironically, they still manage to be loquacious. Almost everything that they say is such an overly dramatic exaggeration anchored by the overly misused word *literally*—"I'm literally dead." I guess *figuratively* doesn't quite have the same flow.

We all have a socially-imposed obligation to follow the same clinical syntax when we communicate; that's why social conversation has become so mundane, and individual styles of communication are so unoriginal. We shamelessly overuse the "it is what it is" tautology, and somehow it's become a bit popular to say *whenever* in place of *when*. We've also gotten really comfortable with using colloquialisms like *conversate* instead of *converse*. I find it particularly irritating when people speak in the second person—as if just because they feel a certain way about something, everyone else must share that same sentiment.

There are infinite words in the English language, yet we continuously recycle the same ones. Many of us refer to certain words as "big words" simply because we don't hear them very often. People like to reinvent a word like *regardless* by adding a nonsensical prefix to turn it into a so-called big word like *irregardless*. There are no big words, just small minds. They say that it's best to remain silent and be thought a fool than to speak and remove all doubt. Too many of us continue to tell on ourselves.

Is Google making us dumber? We substitute our own intelligence for search engines and apps so much that we've developed a dependence on them. Maybe it's just a good thing that we continue to seek knowledge and information. Is it possible that Google is actually making us smarter by making information so easily accessible? Do people read actual, tangible books anymore? The knowledge of social media and technology seems to be more important than the knowledge of math and science. Somehow, it's cooler to be "street smart" than "book smart."

I think that the idea of an "honorary" doctorate is absurd as it diminishes the achievement of those who actually worked hard in a specific field of study to obtain the degree. Just because someone achieves a certain level of success in an outside field of service or entertainment does not make them a "doctor." There are so many people who have a self-imposed imposter syndrome because they want everyone to think that they're smarter or better than they really are. You can't fake an education.

Am I an oxymoronic moron or an idiosyncratic idiot? I can't expect to change social convention with arbitrary semantics. Apparently, I, too, am a victim of the dumbing down of society. You can't take my opinion too seriously; after all, an idiotic intellect is still an idiot.

FABIAN M.C. KUYKENDALL

## *Assault With a Deadly Mind: The Power of Education*

Education is a powerful weapon. You can do a lot more damage with intellect than you can with violence. An educated mind has the wit and the depth of knowledge to destroy haters and trolls with factual truth. Nothing cuts as severely as a scathing indictment of one's true character. The more you know, the more artillery you have.

It was the great Malcolm X who said, "Education is our passport to the future." Since "tomorrow belongs to those who prepare for it today," education is the crucial head start that we all need to live a life of purpose. Education opens doors of opportunity, which lead to endless possibilities. In America, we have the privilege of abundant resources for higher learning. Education is readily available to those who are smart enough to take advantage of it.

Malcolm X also revealed the value of a "homemade education." As evidenced by today's world, you don't need to attend college to succeed. You also don't need to attend college to receive an education. College doesn't work for everyone because everyone absorbs information differently. It takes courage and ambition to think for yourself and find your own path of education. Just as there are infinite things to learn, there are infinite ways to learn them. From Google, YouTube, and Wikipedia to books and post-graduate institutions, our ability to acquire knowledge is an embarrassment of riches.

Many schools, teachers, and parents place sports over education. They teach kids that—along with being a good athlete—winning is the most important thing regarding school. Because sponsors—including parents—donate so much money, schools go out of their way to cater to student athletes with full-ride scholarships and bribes. Even those with poor grades are given a pass and allowed to phone in their education while perpetuating the dumb jock stereotype. Many of the student athletes who make it to the major leagues don't have the education to properly manage their funds and are easily taken advantage of. Without such education, they have nothing to fall back on when their career is over.

On the opposite end, many students are overscheduled, overworked, and forced to overachieve. Some parents and teachers go overboard when it comes to a child's education. They place impossible standards on students, inundating them with more information and activities than they could ever use effectively. After studying in school for seven hours every weekday, they're expected to do up to four hours of homework and squeeze a couple of hours of extracurricular activities in between. Essentially, these children are working full adult-sized days when they haven't developed the physical and emotional capacity to handle such a workload.

School is the most brutal gauntlet in life. Beyond academics, it is a social war zone. The bullying, alienating, and psychological torture lead to an enduring trauma. It's heartbreaking what some kids have to go through just to get an education. Those who survive this gauntlet truly earn their education and the opportunities that come with it. The social education we receive in school is critical in developing our emotional intelligence. As hard as it can be, there's something to learn from every aspect of life.

The acquisition of knowledge is the acquisition of truth. There's power in truth, so—as seekers of knowledge and wisdom—we should always seek truth. We should always be open to learn because no one can ever know everything. We have to learn so that we can teach. Knowledge is useless unless it is passed on to others. Whether teaching a class or teaching others how to treat us, it's essential to be armed with an education.

# CHAPTER 9 - LAW & (IN)JUSTICE

*The Sword, The Scales, & The Lifted Blindfold: The Broken System of Law*

In America, an ever-growing list of cases support the perception that justice is biased, not blind. Justice sees race, religion, political views, and social status. Law and order seems to be about keeping those of a certain class in their place. Because we live in a nation where being Black is probable cause, justice is the exception, not the rule. The blindfold has been removed, blind justice now has perfect vision.

The Supremacy Court is determined to use its Conservative majority to reverse the course of civil rights for race, LGBTQ identity, women's reproduction, and socioeconomic class. Their decisions aren't made for the sake of equality, but for supremacy. In June 2023, the Court overturned affirmative action for college admissions, which was a huge setback for minorities who are easily discriminated against otherwise. So many rich White kids get into universities with their legacy pass, but somehow affirmative action is seen as an "unfair advantage." It's a shame that equality has to be enforced, but, clearly, it does.

Since justice isn't colorblind, it sets different standards when it comes to race. Even in the case of mass shootings, if the killer is Black, he's a "monster;" if the killer is White, he's "mentally ill." It's sickening that even the most contemptuous criminals will still be given the slightest bit of favor if they are White. When Robert Aaron Long shot and killed eight people—including six Asian women—at an Atlanta spa in March 2021, police Capt. Jay Baker downplayed it by saying it "was a really bad day for him." It seems that in almost every case, the White man is privileged with the benefit of the doubt.

In June 2016, Stanford student athlete Brock Turner was sentenced to a mere six months in jail for the sexual assault of an unconscious woman behind a dumpster. This incomprehensibly lenient sentence was given by judge Aaron Persky who felt that "a prison sentence would have a severe impact" on Turner, a champion swimmer. The thing is, he *deserved* to have a severe impact imposed on him—think of the severe impact his actions have on the woman he raped. This is a disturbing case of White privilege. This is White man's justice. What would make a judge believe that anyone should be given preferential treatment despite being a rapist? It's alarming how much sympathy is given to the criminal instead of the actual victim.

The whole court system has become a joke and purely for entertainment. There are numerous court shows on television that produce dramatized faction, making them impossible to take seriously. The fact that shows like *Judge Jerry* and *Judge Steve Harvey* were green-lit highlights a mockery of the justice system. The same can be said for the fact that—in yet another case of White privilege—television actress Lori Loughlin served only two months in prison for her college admissions scam. Meanwhile, there are countless people of color serving life sentences for non-violent crimes.

White tears allowed anti-BLM gunman Kyle Rittenhouse to kill without consequence. Instead, he became a hero to the GOP, NRA, and KKK. If exemptions are made for people like him, why shouldn't mass shooters expect to be able to get away with murder? After countless mass shootings—including the Buffalo hate crime and the Uvalde child massacre—there are still no laws on gun control. The right-wing government has made it glaringly clear that they value guns over innocent lives. These mass shootings aren't going away. How many lives have to be lost before any action is taken?

Every hour, someone dies in a drunk driving collision, so why is America so lenient when it comes to drunk driving? Why is it that when something is so inarguably wrong—such as drunk driving—there's still always pushback when it comes to trying to put an end to it? The current laws only seem to protect the wrong people. When these accidents happen, you always hear about the driver having their 8th or 9th DUI/DWI with no real consequences. How many lives have to be lost before lawmakers change these lax drunk driving laws?

There's a default belief that when someone is imprisoned, they become less than human, and, therefore, deserve to be subjected to dehumanizing conditions. They're starved, beaten, and some are even raped by corrupt prison guards. While criminals most certainly deserve to be punished, it should be understood that their imprisonment *is* their punishment. The law should not allow officers and guards to further this punishment to the extent of torture and suffering.

No good comes from incarceration unless there's rehabilitation. You can't expect to lock a person up for several years then release them back into society without them relapsing into crime. Recidivism is inevitable when a person isn't counseled to understand the reasons behind their criminal ways and how to fix their way of thinking so that they don't re-offend. If we truly want less criminals on the street, we have to *treat* the problem, not just punish it.

Mass incarceration is a reality that disproportionately affects Black men. In fact, there are more Black people in prison today than there were slaves hundreds of years ago. This couldn't possibly be by coincidence, especially considering the fact that America's law enforcement is disproportionately made up of White men. Even Attorney General Jeff Sessions admits, "The office of sheriff is a critical part of the Anglo-American heritage of law enforcement." He goes on to say, "We must never erode this historic office," meaning that White people must make sure that they maintain the upper hand in law. The FBI has long warned about the infiltration of law enforcement agencies by White supremacist groups, yet there continues to be no screening to eliminate candidates with racist, extremist views.

The organization of law enforcement is part of the bigger system of institutional racism. This system ensures that Black people don't get an equal opportunity of justice based on obvious racial prejudice. Black people get harsher punishment for crimes than their White counterparts, and the punishment quite often doesn't fit the crime. Marijuana was legalized in most states, yet countless Black people are still serving time for possession, not to mention all of the wrongly convicted cases of mistaken identity serving time for crimes that they didn't commit. The system is designed for us to fail. The 13$^{th}$ Amendment says that slavery won't exist "except as a punishment for crime;" thus, prison is America's way of keeping Black people enslaved.

When it comes to law enforcement, it seems that fair skin equals fair treatment. There are numerous videos online of White people aggressively resisting arrest, cursing at, and being disrespectful to police officers without punishment, much less losing their lives. Needless to say, the energy of police officers toward Black people is much more hostile and hateful. Who can we depend on for our protection? The American eagle is more protected than a Black person. Much too often, our cases aren't even investigated by police when we lose family members to gun violence because they simply don't care. We don't seem to be worth the effort of them doing their job because—to them—Black lives don't matter.

There are many police officers who carelessly exchange racist memes and posts on social media, making it abundantly clear that they don't view each race equally. A racist mind given a badge of the law is extremely dangerous. Is it the least bit possible that these are the type of officers who—without hesitation—shoot to kill unarmed Black men with raised hands, who are pinned to the ground, or are completely innocent? Are these the type of officers who would ever give a Black man a fair chance? Their racially motivated interest in law makes it impossible for them to do their job ethically.

In March 2021, a North Carolina police officer arrested a six-year-old Black boy for picking a tulip. Which part of that last sentence makes any sense? What this officer did was rob this young child of his innocence. His intention was to ingrain into this young Black mind that he isn't anything more than a criminal, nor will he ever be. The pure evil displayed by members of our law enforcement is so commonplace that no one seems to give it a second thought anymore.

Officers continue to get away with their crimes against humanity because there's no one to police the police. Even with all of the constant glaring evidence, no one is willing to entertain the notion that there is a serious problem here. The problem seems to be the culture and the system that is American law enforcement. This is a culture that trains its members to turn a blind eye to racial injustices, and a system that punishes its members if they don't, therefore eliminating the potential for any actual good cops. On top of that, the cops involved in these injustices are rarely properly prosecuted because judges don't want to "make an example" out of them. These judges don't want the officers to pay for other officers' crimes, so their crimes are acquitted, and the cycle continues.

Psychological and ethical examination needs to be done more thoroughly *before* one is given the power of enforcing law. Why is it that members of law enforcement aren't required to go to *law* school? If they don't have a proficient understanding of the law, why should they be allowed to enforce it? The band-aid approach isn't going to fix what is obviously broken, the system needs to be completely restructured. By no means should systemic racism be allowed in law enforcement, so why is it? Not only does the prison system need a total reform, but the entire justice system needs to be reformed as well. Rather than "defund the police," we need to *restructure* the police. We can't just keep saying, "fuck the system," we have to figure out how to *change* the system.

It's pretty sad that there's even a need for law enforcement to wear body cameras, but because they abuse their power and engage in corruption so frequently, extra measures of protection have become necessary. I believe that anyone who is given such a position of power should also be required to have a certain level of transparency when he or she is on the job. It's about accountability. During the insurrection of our nation's Capitol, there were alt-right radical White supremacist cops who assisted in that shameful act of terrorism. Unsurprisingly, few of them have had to atone for their betrayal because White privilege *trumps* accountability.

It's no conspiracy when I say that the lawmen who enforce a war on drugs are the same ones who created the need for this so-called war. This is the type of government compliance responsible for the '80s-'90s crack epidemic. Basically, they incarcerate Black people for using and selling the drugs and guns that they plant in our neighborhoods. They litter these low-income areas with their poison to juice the American economy (along with their own pockets) while we end up killing ourselves—two birds with one stone.

For everything that they've done to us—and for everything that they continue to do to us—America owes all Black people restorative justice in the form of reparations. From what I understand, America has issued some degree of restitution to Native people, but what has this country done to reconcile its history with Black people? The famous allusion of forty acres and a mule was never intended to be brought to fruition, only to play in our faces. It's a disgrace that Black people would probably have to file suit against the American government to have them acknowledge their wrongdoings toward us.

Every year, there are states that implement new voting laws to make it harder for certain demographics to vote. Their Jim Crow agenda uses voter suppression to eliminate supposed voter fraud. There's an ongoing practice of changing laws to benefit one very specific group of people. These biased, partisan laws reflect the broken legal system. We've grown too accustomed to allowing these miscarriages of justice. The fact is, unless there's justice for all, there is no justice.

## *Justified Injustice: America's War on "Thugs"*

The word *thug* has become—for conservative White America—a guiltless substitute for the word *nigger*. Apparently, there aren't any White thugs. All thugs seem to be Black men who pose a serious danger to all of mankind, and, therefore, must be eradicated.

America's police officers are at war on their own soil. Somehow, it serves their country—and brings them honor—to annihilate the Black enemy. These officers are hunting Black people down like human game. Eventually, they'll be mounting our heads like trophies on their walls. Maybe we're not good for the ecosystem, maybe our population is getting out of control. Maybe that's why we have to be poached, to bring order back to biodiversity. Essentially, police are paid to kill Black people.

Police have become licensed terrorists, allowed to profile not only Black people, but Hispanic people, Asian people, and those whom they perceive to be Muslims as well. These officers demand—especially from minorities—unmitigated servility, which they're likely to sugarcoat with a word like *respect*. However, it's not just about respect; they want us to fear them the way that they fear us. They have this "negrophobic," fear-based hatred toward us, which is inexplicably justified based on their own stereotypes. For them, the greatest threat to White supremacy is the Black man.

The systemic racism that erodes our law enforcement allows bigoted White people—who barely hide their racism behind their badges—to target and kill Black people. Most disturbingly, these killings are lawful at their discretion, and the officers are often acquitted due to statutory language. These killers know how to play the game of a system that was designed to work in their favor. That's why they always make sure to mention that the Black male victim was a perceived "threat," that he appeared to "reach for a gun," and that they "feared for (their) life." How does every Black man "fit the description" of a criminal?

American law enforcement is a national gang founded upon the principles of Aryan brotherhood. Their mission appears to be Black genocide. It's obvious that some people become cops solely to enforce the oppression of Black people.

It's gotten to a point where any Black person who "looks threatening" or "acts suspiciously" or "resists authority" is no longer human and is dealt with accordingly. This is blatant, deliberate racism that is continuously justified with ignorant excuses and outright lies. Only callous, apathetic arrogance would expect us to believe that in every case of a Black man gunned down by police, he was reaching for a gun that never existed.

Cops and politicians have blamed these killings on the excuse that Black people don't know how to properly interact with police. It sounds like every single White person in America is just better behaved or better trained than we are; therefore, they get to keep their lives. There was a time when people who didn't properly interact with police were arrested; now—if they're Black—they're killed, no remorse, no apology, no humanity. To say that Black people bring these murders upon ourselves due to our lack of unwavering obedience to law enforcement is such a convenient lie. Meanwhile, many visibly armed White criminals not only aren't killed—or even shot at—by police, but the use of force isn't even applied by police to apprehend them. The convenient lie serves only to excuse and legalize the elimination of Black people.

Why is it that officers who have been trained to handle these situations can never seem to deescalate them without killing yet another Black person? Why is it so easy for law enforcement officials—and their mostly White supporters—to have such cavalier, dismissive reactions to these injustices? Do the corrupt officers cater to the large portion of White America who treat them as heroes for their service as villains? Whether you're in law enforcement or you're one of their staunch supporters, you're well aware of the long history of racist behavior by law enforcement—and the countless documented, publicized, and televised cases of such behavior—so you can't insult our intelligence by pretending that it doesn't exist.

There is a killer cop culture that seems to have become the training model for law enforcement in America. Officers seem to have an expectation to be able to kill at will, no questions asked. It happens so frequently—and has been so normalized—that most Black people have come to expect that no ethical officers exist. Police have a code of silence which suggests that "good" officers must never speak out against their evil brothers and sisters. However, a good officer would condemn—not condone—corrupt behavior. A good officer wouldn't stand by idly and watch as their fellow officers murder yet another innocent human being.

It's sad how numb we've become to stories about unarmed Black people being killed—in public and often on video—by officers. These stories aren't even shocking anymore, it's no longer news. The world has been so desensitized to this kind of violence that many people casually post images and videos of murders on social media. When these incidents happen, there always seems to be witnesses, but the problem with society is that people would rather film an injustice than do something about it.

Police have a habit of "accidentally" shooting and killing Black people like Breonna Taylor and Daunte Wright. Most times, they scramble to dig up a criminal background to justify the murder, and—per usual—they get away with it. Why are all of these "oops" police killings of Black people so easily excusable? For many White people, there's always a justification for why Black people are killed by police, even before they know the facts. This seems to be the collective attitude of those who "back the badge." Too many of them are convinced that police can do no wrong as long as they continue to rid the world of the niggers they call "thugs."

When we say, "Black lives matter," they say, "blue lives matter." However, blue lives are predominately White lives who *chose* to be blue; Black lives aren't afforded that same choice. We are seen as negatively Black regardless of circumstance or uniform, while so-called blue lives exercise White power. The "thin blue line" brigade seems to think that blue lives matter because they put an end to so many Black lives. The phrase "blue lives matter" was only created to mock the Black Lives Matter movement. However, we all know damn well that if White people were being targeted and killed by police officers on a recurring basis, there would be an outcry far louder than there ever was.

Police officers—and their loyal Conservative following—have branded themselves as the victims in this war on thugs, which they created. After all of the blood on their hands, they still cry out for sympathy so that they can be terrorists *and* saviors. It seems that police want government and community support for killing Black people. They claimed that the Derek Chauvin verdict set a "bad precedent" for policing in America. The conviction of the monster and coward who lynched George Floyd was somehow an injustice in their eyes. These corrupt cops are, indeed, the thugs that they accuse us of being.

It often feels like Black officers are in support of what seems to be the White officers' agenda: unjustly enslaving and eradicating Black people. They seem to have a self-hate that prevents them from understanding that—even while covered in blue—they're still Black. They can turn a blind eye to—or even participate in—the killing of their own people, but their colleagues will still only see them as niggers in uniform. The five Black officers who brutally beat Tyre Nichols to death were almost immediately charged with murder. I hate to think of the lighter circumstances they might have faced if they were White.

Police officers are hired and trained to protect and serve. Somehow, this seems to include being able to pick and choose whom they protect and serve. These are supposed professionals who have been entrusted with a serious position of authority. They are held to a higher moral standard than everyday civilians, so any breech of that code is completely unacceptable. Some districts have started to require that their officers take racial sensitivity courses. Any step in the right direction is good; however, I struggle with my optimism in this regard. I find it disconcerting that officers who have already been deemed qualified enough to hire now have to learn Black history and be taught that we're actually people too.

It's a shame that the hateful actions of corrupt officers lead many Black people to believe that all officers share that same hate. Most Black people simply don't trust police because they feel like they have no reason to. I don't doubt that there are ethical police officers in this country, but why don't more of them speak out against the corrupt ones? When Black people speak out against police brutality and injustice, why is that taken as an attack on *all* police officers? It really says a lot that simply asking to be treated fairly is considered to be anti-police.

America's war on thugs is certainly nothing new. Police brutality has been a racist release for White supremacist cops for decades. Rodney King became a poster child for police brutality when he was videotaped being severely beaten by officers of the Los Angeles Police Department in 1991. The LAPD—infamous for its history of police brutality—routinely used the term "No Humans Involved" (NHI) in reference to the murders of Black people. I can't get over the irony of inhumane people treating us as if we're less than human. This is the kind of sick, soulless evil that has become standard in American law enforcement.

The war on thugs is the catalyst for the race war of this era. As officers continue to gun down Black people, it unfortunately leads to revenge attacks on law enforcement. In July 2016, Micah Xavier Johnson shot and killed five police officers in Dallas. This was an unthinkable response to the police killings of Alton Sterling and Philando Castile. As a Black man, I feel like these actions are counter-productive to the movement toward justice. It's not about an eye for an eye because hate can never conquer hate. Bullets can't speak for us. Instead, we have to trust that as long as we continue to use our voices, we will be heard.

Revenge attacks are pointless. They only give the corrupt officers what they want: a war. These officers seem to have the mindset that we—Black men—are the enemy, and that they're at war with us. A revenge attack only makes them feel like they have a valid reason to keep profiling us and gunning us down. I'll never understand how they can take lives so casually and still live with themselves. What keeps me going is knowing that God sees all, and every evil deed that went unnoticed will eventually be punished in the name of karma.

To every hateful murderer in a police costume: You deserve every sleepless night you have and every second of guilt you feel. It's a shame that your children and family—by association—also have to suffer from your ignorant actions. It's pathetic that your mind is so weak that a Black man's existence can make you feel powerless, forcing you to kill him so that you can feel like a man. God saw what you did, and He knows exactly what your intentions were. The white camouflage of Amerikkka won't hide you from Him. Your day of reckoning is inevitable.

Systemic racism has become epidemic racism. Black people are treated as terrorists in America. To call us all "thugs" is to justify an injustice. Whether criminal or vigilante, vagabond or executive, sinner or saint, we are human. This war on thugs is a war on humanity.

## *Witch Hunt: The Court of Public Opinion*

There is no due process in the court of public opinion. No one gets a fair trial, just an instant indictment. Everyone loves a witch hunt. Humans are like sheep and have a herd mentality. It's much easier to go along with the herd than to be the black sheep by going your own way. For the love of casting condemnation, we form lynch mobs and hunt people down with torches and pitch forks.

The jury is larger and louder than ever thanks to social media. An ever-growing number of people are becoming victims of social media sentencing in the name of cancel culture. Most times, it doesn't matter if they deserve it or not; they're accused regardless of fact or fiction. It's becoming almost acceptable to convict someone based on a lie and for everyone to hop on that bandwagon for the sake of the witch hunt. According to Charlamagne tha God—co-host of radio show *The Breakfast Club*—no one cares about the truth when the lie is more entertaining.

Entertainment media and social media love to dig up the skeletons of a person's past in order to vilify or criminalize them. In the court of public opinion, no one is given a fair trial, particularly Black men. Black men are guilty until proven *not* guilty, never innocent. If a Black man is guilty in his past, he's guilty indefinitely. Many noted celebrities—like hip-hop legend Jay-Z—have consistently dealt with their past being brought up in order to cast shade on their accomplishments.

When Jay-Z received his first Album of the Year Grammy nomination for 2017's *4:44*, we were again reminded by biased media outlets that he was once a drug dealer. Similarly, when Kobe Bryant won an Academy Award in 2018 for his animated short film *Dear Basketball*, the media quickly dragged his 2003 sexual assault case back to the surface. The way the media and society sees it, a Black man is incapable of positive change. Even if he becomes a multi-billionaire rapper and mogul or an Oscar-winning basketball icon, if he makes a mistake, he *is* that mistake.

Be it good or bad, the legend of Michael Jackson seems to be immortal. Although he was widely celebrated before and after his passing, there have been countless campaigns to destroy his image and tarnish his legacy. They hate to hear it, but when a person of staggering success and greatness is also Black, it doesn't sit well with a lot of people. Even though the many accusations against Jackson were never proven, a certain sector of the public had already made up its mind and chose to criminalize him. Even years after his death, new accusations have arisen against a man who can't even defend himself. It goes without saying that Jackson was—at least—as flawed as the rest of us. He had eccentricities that many of us could never understand, but it's unfair to use that to excoriate him.

When it comes to public opinion on celebrity misdoings, there's a lot of selective outrage. Because Rock and Roll legends like Elvis Presley and Jerry Lee Lewis were so perfectly White, their sins are largely ignored. People conveniently forget that Presley was involved with future wife Priscilla when she was only 14 and that Lewis married his 13-year-old cousin. In a world of double standards for race, these men could do no wrong; thus, their beatification. The public is always quick to forgive bigots like Mel Gibson, Paula Deen, Michael Richards, Dog the Bounty Hunter, and Hulk Hogan. There's never any lasting consequences for their racist actions, just excuses and acceptance.

It's become evident that there are racist blackballers in the entertainment industry who use their positions of power to control—mainly Black—celebrities. When pop icon Janet Jackson had that infamous wardrobe malfunction at the 2004 Super Bowl, her music was blacklisted by then-CEO of Viacom Leslie Moonves and her career suffered. Meanwhile, singer Justin Timberlake was hardly held accountable for his role in the incident. His White male privilege got him through the backlash relatively unscathed, leaving Jackson—the Black female—to endure the brunt of the punishment. The court of public opinion made this double standard exceedingly clear.

Singer Chris Brown was blocked from performance opportunities over a decade after his domestic abuse incident against fellow singer Rihanna. Rapper Nicki Minaj was basically blacklisted from ever receiving a Grammy Award after her controversial performance at the 2012 ceremony. When artists like Minaj and Ms. Jackson don't allow themselves to be controlled by those in power, they suffer the consequences of not kneeling down and kissing the ring. The powers that be, apparently, will never stop punishing them for their past mistakes. All it takes is one move in the wrong direction to be unfairly subjected to double jeopardy.

People live for the opportunity to judge, that's why they're always looking for the moral high ground. The world is overrun with social justice warriors, pretentious vigilantes, and those who attempt to be judge, jury, and executioner. When someone is brought to trial to have their character judged by society, they are at their most vulnerable, which entices the public to pounce. As evidence of the history of mankind's bloodlust, people have been burned at the stake, lynched, decapitated, and crucified all in front of a bloodthirsty audience. People take pleasure in the misfortune of others and judge them with self-righteous hypocrisy. While it's easy to condemn others for their crimes, the Bible says, "judge not, lest ye be judged."

The court of public opinion is much like the court of law, it's completely biased and unfair. For the fiendishly sententious masses, the only fitting sentence for crimes of morality is capital punishment. Society is a grand jury that's always on jury duty. However, in the case of the people vs. impartial justice, the jury's out. Every knee-jerk indictment leads to an inevitable mistrial. Our censorious society has proved to be unfit for law. Ultimately, only God can judge.

# CHAPTER 10 - HEALTH & MEDICINE

*The Wealth of Health: A Lifestyle of Wellness*

Personal health comprises mind, body, and spirit. It is a lifestyle that plays a vital role in our overall quality of life. A healthy lifestyle requires the right diet, activity, and mentality. Ultimately, in order to live healthy, you have to want to live.

It starts with feeding our minds with food for thought. The power of positive thinking helps us overcome any mental obstacle that stands in the way of our wellness. We must never underestimate the power of words and remember that what we tell ourselves, we eventually believe. If we say that we can't, then we won't, so why not be optimistic? Positive thoughts and affirmations are the salve that aid in our mental wellness.

As they say, you are what you eat; therefore, we should eat for nourishment, not pleasure. Food is neither entertainment nor therapy. We have to proactively deal with our feelings instead of eating them. It often seems like we ingest toxins no matter what we eat. When we live to eat, we become prisoners of obesity. When you're obese, ironically, you're seen as less of a person. What's worse is that you start to see yourself the same way. When we eat to live, we create long lives of health and happiness. Our bodies are temples and should be respected with premium upkeep.

Exercise puts life into our bodies. It gives us a rush of endorphins that makes us feel as good as we could ever feel. It also makes us look good, which is a popular motivation. We all want to look good because, again, it makes us feel good. When you are blessed with the privilege of having an able body, it is your humble responsibility to utilize it to its full capacity and not take it for granted. We have to continue to move or else—sooner than later—we'll stop moving forever.

Sleep is the restoration and replenishment that's essential for our bodies. It's the daily recharge that gives us the energy that we need to function in our lives. It should go without saying, but ingesting toxins like drugs and alcohol are detrimental to our well-being. To relieve pain and stress, there are natural remedies like Cannabidiol (CBD) products. Herbal medicine, vitamins, and supplements help us cleanse our bodies and guard against illness in a safe, all-natural way.

Health is directly connected to spirituality. Whatever your spiritual path is, it's important to practice mindfulness and meditation. Many of us don't even realize the therapeutic benefits of deep, focused breathing. When our chakras are in alignment, their energy harmonizes our mind, body, and spirit. We all feel a spiritual connection to either God, the universe, or nature. Whether it's through religion or yoga, we mustn't neglect the higher power that gives us guidance in life.

It often feels like aging is a curse. No one wants to get older because it's bad for your health and it takes away your youth. Remember that health *is* youth, it makes you live longer. It's a currency that buys you more time and a better quality of life. Laughing, socializing, and dwelling exclusively in positive energy are crucial to having a happy, healthy life. It isn't health that makes you happy, it's happiness that makes you healthy.

## *21ˢᵗ Century Genocide: The Cure & The Kill in Medicine*

Since the dawning of the 21ˢᵗ century, there has been a serious opioid epidemic. Although there are many factors that have contributed to this, I think that most manufacturers knowingly mislead consumers to believe that its drugs are safe and without the risk of dangerous addiction. I also think that a lot of doctors are egregiously irresponsible with their prescribing of these drugs. Ultimately, the big business of capitalism is to blame.

Mallinckrodt Pharmaceuticals played a substantial role in the opioid crisis, flooding the country with hundreds of millions of pills and contributing to over 14,000 overdose deaths in 2013 alone. In 2018, former Florida doctor Barry Schultz was sentenced to 157 years in prison for drug trafficking, operating a cash-only opioid "pill mill" out of his office. Schultz prescribed tens of thousands of narcotic pills to patients who didn't even need them, resulting in countless overdoses. This drug lord and killer insists that he was trying to help his patients when he clearly was helping himself to millions of dollars at their expense.

In August 2016, well-known herbal healer Dr. Sebi passed away. It is believed by many of his followers that he was killed because his natural remedies for serious illnesses were a threat to Big Pharma. There's a conspiracy theory that holistic doctors have developed cures for many diseases—including cancer and AIDS—and that these doctors have been silenced by means of death so that their breakthroughs don't drain the money pit of the global pharmaceutical industry.

Tobacco companies are blatantly marketing to children. They're selling vaping hoodies and candy-flavored vaping pens in bright cartoon colors with a toy-like aesthetic. They're also targeting young women by producing vaping pens with fashionable, cosmetic designs. Trying to make vaping look influencer-trendy is one thing, but intentionally trying to get children to vape is deplorable and should be criminal. The chemicals ingested through a vaping device have proved to be just as harmful and addictive as those in cigarettes, yet vaping is marketed as a safer alternative to smoking. It's clear that the health effects of tobacco products will always take a back seat to their profits.

The healthcare industry is tainted with too many stories of unethical practices. There have been reports of hospitals concealing prices from their patients, hitting them with surprise bills, or billing them twice for the same visit. They routinely overmedicate patients with reckless disregard for the possible consequences. It's troubling how often we hear about senior abuse and neglect in the industry. Healthcare workers in assisted living facilities made a specific choice to dedicate their lives and careers to taking care of our most vulnerable loved ones, so I don't understand why so many of them inflict intentional harm.

It's terrifying to know that some doctors have prejudiced views toward some of their patients. Because of a doctor's aversion to their race, gender, sexuality, or religion, for some people, seeking treatment could be more dangerous than not. Black people tend to avoid and mistrust doctors more than other races. The reason for this goes as far back as the 40-year Tuskegee Experiment, which began in 1932. Our very own U.S. Public Health Service conducted a nefarious study on hundreds of Black men under the guise of free medical care. The actual purpose of the study was to observe the effects of untreated syphilis in Black men, who were used as unsuspecting human guinea pigs. Not only were the men not told that they had syphilis, the PHS never treated them for the disease, resulting in—at least—128 deaths.

There's a racist myth that Black people have a higher tolerance for pain than other races. As scary as it is, many doctors seem to subscribe to this ridiculous notion. Their belief can likely be traced back to the antebellum period when slave masters performed horrific experimental surgeries on their slaves without anesthesia. This practice evolved into doctors enforcing birth control on Black women in prisons in the form of sterilization after labor and injecting them with "human pesticides." Because many doctors acquired the legacy of seeing Black people as less than human, they've treated us as living cadavers.

Studies have shown that Black people tend to endure physical "weathering" from prolonged exposure to stress and racism. What doesn't help is the fact that medical treatment in Black communities is generally substandard. As Black people make up the majority of residents in inner-city neighborhoods in this country, it makes it easy for some health professionals to give us differential treatment. Too many of them seem to be apathetic to our condition simply based on medical racism. Their cultural incompetence even has them racializing diseases to our detriment. Sometimes, the ones who are supposed to help us, hurt us. Sometimes, the ones who are supposed to cure us, kill us.

There has been a lot of talk about mandating the presence of video cameras in the operating room. Personally, this is something that I would prefer if I ever needed surgical treatment. I think that it's important for doctors—who hold a lot of power—to have a layer of transparency and accountability in the event that something goes wrong. There are also many people in the medical field who engage in malpractice. From leaving surgical utensils inside a patient's body to inappropriate sexual behavior when a patient is under anesthesia, these medical professionals clearly present the need for patient protection. For everyone's safety and security, cameras in the operating room should become a necessity.

I believe that many people become doctors for the purpose of using their position to violate patients under the guise of medical care. Doctors like the disgraced Larry Nassar feel entitled to abuse their power and exercise their perversions. Most doctors who practice gynecology and proctology seem to be driven by fetishism. They seem to have an unnatural obsession with probing and essentially raping their patients. I can't help but wonder why one would devote their lives to studying random ani.

When the Covid vaccine became available to the public, it was subject to illogical conspiracy theories by radical anti-vaxers. A Wisconsin pharmacist deliberately sabotaged more than 500 doses of the vaccine, believing that it could harm people and "change their DNA." People carelessly spread vaccine misinformation and came up with self-prescribed Covid remedies. Popular podcast host Joe Rogan—having no medical background—convinced millions of his gullible followers that the anti-parasitic drug ivermectin could give them Covid immunity. We truly are the biggest threat to our own health.

It's infuriating how a government forces you to buy health insurance—whether you want it or not—based on what they feel is affordable for you, while knowing nothing of your expenses. Just because you earn a decent amount of money doesn't mean that you can automatically afford to pay these overpriced monthly premiums, especially when you already pay countless other bills, fees, and loans every month. You almost have to hope that some severe medical issue arises just to make your health insurance worthwhile.

The bottom line is, you're paying for a "what if." What the government doesn't understand is that not every person operates that way. Not every person has a family to protect with insurance. Not every person feels the need to pay for a service that they don't even use. Some people would rather have health care on an as-needed basis, and I believe that they should have that option. No one should be forced to buy insurance—or be charged with a ridiculous penalty if they don't—just to satisfy the greed of a shameless government.

America is severely overmedicated. It seems that most medication does more harm than good. We even need medication to combat the side effects of medication. Even with all of this medication and medical advancements, for some diseases, there will never be a cure. There's no money in the cure, the money is in the medicine.

## *Dirty Until Proven Clean: Sports' Doping Epidemic*

The world of sports has been tainted by a doping epidemic. Use of performance-enhancing drugs (PEDs) has taken center field in many a scandal. There have been reports of doping in baseball, track and field, cycling, swimming, tennis, wrestling, football, figure skating, and gymnastics, among other sports. For that reason, sports can never be viewed the same way again.

The BALCO scandal of 2003 shed light on the company that had supplied undetectable PEDs to professional athletes since the '80s. Victor Conte—founder and president of BALCO—was the steroid drug lord who helped develop tetrahydrogestrinone (THG) and aided in the corruption of sports. In what seemed like an effort to excuse his behavior, he told *20/20,* "The whole history of the (Olympic) games is just full of corruption, cover-up, and performance-enhancing drug use." The BALCO scandal exposed many high-profile athletes including Barry Bonds, Marion Jones, Jason Giambi, Shane Mosley, and Bill Romanowski.

Other famous juicers include Lance Armstrong, Mark McGwire, and Jose Canseco. Because they cheated, their accomplishments have been erased from history, they've been stripped of their titles, and their glory has been replaced with shame. These athletes ultimately sacrifice their health due to the long-term effects of steroid use, which include heart failure, high blood pressure, high cholesterol, liver disease, and cancer. It goes to show the lengths that some athletes will go to for the thrill of victory and to avoid the agony of defeat.

Russia has a long, infamous history of cheating. Over 200 of their athletes have been caught doping at the Olympics, and they've been stripped of almost 50 Olympic medals. They've also been banned from international competition and only allowed to compete at the Olympics under the flag of the Russian Olympic Committee (ROC). Russia has had a state-sponsored doping program, much like East Germany in the 1970s, whose system forced many of its athletes to use steroids—often said to be "vitamins"—in an attempt to prove communist superiority. The East German women's swim team experienced virilization in the form of heavy musculature, facial hair, and deepened voice, for which they were ridiculed. Many also suffered miscarriages due to steroid use.

At the 1988 Olympic Games in Seoul, South Korea, Canadian sprinter Ben Johnson set a world record in the men's 100 meters, winning the gold medal over American rival—and track & field legend—Carl Lewis. Johnson was later stripped of his gold medal and his world record after testing positive for—and later admitting to using—an anabolic steroid. Lewis was subsequently awarded the gold medal. Johnson was shamed, his legacy was tarnished, and his Olympic moment went down in infamy. Regarding the fallout, International Olympic Committee member Anita DeFrantz said, "The games are to be a celebration of human excellence, not of medical superiority."

Lewis once insinuated that fellow track legend Usain Bolt may have had the assistance of PEDs due to his stellar performance at the 2008 Olympic Games. Even if the thought was understandable, the veiled accusation was inappropriate and unfair. Lewis actually cast aspersions on the whole Jamaican athletics program by alluding to lax doping controls being a factor in their success while adding, "I'm not saying they've done anything for certain. I don't know." Given that Lewis himself has tested positive for stimulants multiple times in his career, he knows firsthand how it feels to come under heavy scrutiny. He should also know how unfair it is to prematurely indict an athlete—while not knowing their medical status—and rob them of their moment of glory. It's a shame that—because of the actions of cheaters—innocent athletes will have to deal with the presumption of guilt.

Tennis legend Serena Williams and gymnastics GOAT Simone Biles both had their medical information leaked by Russian hackers trying to destroy their careers. Upset and perplexed by how two Black women could be so dominant in their respective sports, the group had to conclude that it was because of PEDs. It was later revealed that Williams used anti-inflammatories to treat muscle injuries and that Biles used Ritalin to treat ADHD, both of which were approved by the World Anti-Doping Agency. The hackers tried to discredit these women—and the U.S.—out of hateful spite. Their desperate attempt at sabotage failed.

It's worth noting that some athletes suffer harsh consequences for doping, even when they're completely unaware of it. At the 2000 Olympic Games in Sydney, Australia, Romanian gymnast Andreea Raducan tested positive for pseudoephedrine from a cold suppressant given to her by a team doctor. Even though the medicine gave her no athletic advantage, it still contained a banned substance, and she was stripped of her all-around gold medal. It's unfair that minors are at the mercy of adult doctors on whom they have to rely to receive the appropriate (legal) medication.

When an athlete uses PEDs, it not only tarnishes their sport, it presents an unfair obstacle for their clean competitors. Athletes deserve the right to know that they're competing on a level playing field. Besides being unethical, doping is an embarrassing act of desperation. I don't understand how anyone can feel like a winner while knowing that they cheated to do so. It seems that most cheaters have the attitude of, "If everyone else is doing it, then all is fair." Why is winning a game or an event worth more than your integrity? Why does it define your self-worth? The "win at all costs" mentality is disturbing. The spirit of sport is dead.

It's widely believed that doping in sports went on for decades before it was made public. It was even said to have been acceptable at one point in time. It makes you wonder how many past champions were actually clean. Now, anytime someone sets a new world record in the 100 meters or breaks the record for home runs, their accomplishment will be put into question. There will be a permanent asterisk in the history books robbing these accomplishments of their authenticity. From now on, anyone who achieves an extraordinary feat of sport will presumably be dirty until proven clean. Sports will never be the same again.

## *Defective: The Stigma of Mental Illness*

People who suffer from mental illness are often treated like pariahs or lepers. They're looked at as defective human beings. As ridiculous as it is, mental illness is still taboo, even though it affects everybody. We all know someone with mental health issues, and—to some degree—we all have mental health issues. Why aren't we as serious about our mental health as we are about our physical health? Many insurance companies don't even cover mental health care. Sadly, many healthcare professionals seem to have a blasé attitude about treating mental illness. Why are doctors so quick to medicate mental illness instead of dealing with the deeper issues that cause it?

A big problem in our society is that many people don't believe in mental illness. They assume that everyone has a choice in how they act and react. They're obliviously insensitive to other people's mental impairments, often dismissing them as "crazy." However, they also use the word *crazy* to describe any person with eccentricities who doesn't fit into what's considered normal, unable to distinguish true psychosis and neurosis. They don't understand that mental illness is a real thing that can't be cured with a pill, and they don't care unless it affects them personally.

Every day, we walk through a video game labyrinth of triggers that we have to dodge. We have to deal with incessant politics, the rising threat of civil and nuclear war, social media pathology, and the constant, inescapable bad news spread by every media outlet. I believe that social media has given everyone a mental illness to some extent. It's not normal. It's unrealistic and it imposes ridiculous expectations. Sometimes, we need to unplug and disconnect from this delirious world. The world—as it is—is not conducive to sanity.

In the Black community, we inherit race-related mental illness. The stress, anxiety, and depression that we experience draws a direct parallel to the trauma of slavery. This makes us more susceptible than other races to mental diseases like Alzheimer's. Too many people in the Black community don't believe in counseling and therapy, choosing, instead, to believe that mental illness is just a temporary bad mood and that we can go to church and pray it away. We have to change our way of thinking and stop being too proud to acknowledge and support our mental health.

Somehow, the consensus assumes that we're all born with a *normal* mental capacity that some of us simply choose to go against. Because society feels that it shouldn't have sympathy for stigmatized people, those with psychosexual disorders like pedophilia almost never seek treatment for their disease out of fear and shame. Instead, they attempt to hide or suppress their disease, and, without treatment, they end up committing crimes that possibly could have been prevented. Having a mental illness doesn't forgive criminal behavior, but—at the very least—these people need and deserve help.

In recent years, we've finally opened up a global mental health conversation, and we've begun to normalize mental health care. At the Tokyo Olympics in 2021, Simone Biles—widely acknowledged as the greatest and most decorated gymnast of all time—made history for *not* competing. Going into these Olympics, she was already heralded as the star of the games and expected to win the most gold medals. Even though she had proved many times that she could handle such massive pressure, this time, her mind finally had enough.

She chose to bow out of the team competition after suffering a dangerous mind/body disconnect known as the "twisties," which causes one to lose perception of where they are in the air. Although many applauded and supported her decision, a more radically political demographic castigated and vilified her as an un-American "quitter." I say to them: If winning a gold medal is so important to you, why don't you squeeze your fat ass into a leotard and do an Amanar on the vault. In America, the world of sports has shown itself to have no room or sympathy for mental health issues; the most important thing will always be winning. At the 2020 Olympics, however, Simone Biles decided that she didn't owe anyone any more gold medals, and she chose to put her mental health first.

Unfortunately, most of us don't think about what poor mental health can lead to. Personality and mood disorders like depression, anxiety, and bi-polar disorder can cause people to believe that suicide is the only solution. People who commit suicide don't want to end their lives, they want to *change* their lives, and, sadly, suicide seems like the easiest way to do so. We have to realize that we are not alone in the way that we feel so that we can free ourselves from suffering in silence. We've all heard that it's okay not to be okay, which means that it's okay to ask for help. We also have to be willing to help each other.

So, "How are you?" Most of us who ask people this question don't really care about the answer. We always expect to hear the typical response of "fine" or "good/well." We've also grown accustomed to giving such responses when asked, but what if we felt safe enough to be honest? What if we had the empathy and compassion that made people feel welcome to open up emotionally? It's hard for us to see it in the moment, but we can actually save someone's life just by listening to them. Depression makes us feel like no one cares, but sometimes we don't even realize when we're depressed. Too many of us don't take the time to assess how we feel. When we're able to have a meaningful conversation with someone about our mental state, we allow ourselves to heal.

It's so important that we protect our mental health. We have to be careful of what we allow into our mental space because whatever gets in there will only grow. Sometimes, it's necessary for us to take a break from people, places, or situations that trigger negative mindsets. What we all should know by now is that mental illness is real and it should be treated as an utmost priority. We have to destigmatize mental illness because—in the end—it's something from which we all suffer.

# CHAPTER 11 - ECONOMICS & FINANCE

---

### *Bulls & Bears: Chasing The American Scheme*

The American dream was once idealized as a white picket fenced envy-green grass suburban aspiration. Today, it has come to represent an affluent life of greed and excess. It's all about the accumulation of wealth and toys, e.g., yachts, private jets, luxury cars, and other mid-life crisis clichés. Hard work isn't valued as much as instant wealth. Many people find it more worthwhile to pursue a "get rich quick" pipe dream than to gradually build upon a sure thing. The world teaches us that money buys happiness and that it's okay to acquire it by any means. As life is a gamble, we spin the wheel of fortune at our own risk.

We shamelessly glorify money. Many of us use it to fill a soulless void. We're trained to believe that our wealth is our worth, the value of life that defines us. We measure success based on the amount of money and material possessions we have. Most people seem to want wealth for the sake of feeling superior to those who don't have it. It gives them license to look down on those who are lower in class. They make the money so that it can make *them*, hoping to cover the fact that they're less than what they seem to be. Rather than use their wealth to help the less fortunate, they hold on to every dollar and cent just to maintain their position on the Forbes list; that's the stupidity of cupidity.

Capitalism in the '80s taught us that "greed is good." The film *Wall Street* inspired a generation of stockbrokers, venture capitalists, corporate raiders, and Gordon Gekko-worshiping yuppies. These white-collar carnivores are a part of the everyday rat race, fighting to climb the corporate ladder and stepping on each other's necks to get to the top. The actual Wall Street is the world's hub for stocks and bonds, supply and demand, and buying and selling for bulls and bears. It's where the one percent gather to fulfill their pursuit of the almighty dollar through unscrupulous ambition. It's expected—even required—for you to plot and scheme your way to the top of the pyramid. What is it about money that makes us such avaricious gluttons? Everyone wants their piece of the pie, but we want everyone else's as well.

When cryptocurrency became trendy, payment systems like Bitcoin gave users new ways to invest—and potentially lose—lots of money. Cryptocurrency has often been compared to a pyramid scheme or money laundering. Non-fungible tokens (NFTs)—which also gained inexplicable popularity—presented yet another intangible asset to be sold and traded. The NFT market has often been compared to an economic bubble or a Ponzi scheme and has frequently been used in scams. People are always quick to jump on board what they think is an easy opportunity to accumulate wealth, that's why millions engage in stock market gambling. Wall Street is Las Vegas for corporate sharks.

The sharks on TV's *Shark Tank* sit smugly on their thrones as start-up entrepreneurs present their ideas in hopes to receive financial backing. The contestants have no aversion to begging a panel of egotistical billionaires for money, and the sharks have no qualms about making the contestants roll over and jump through hoops before hitting them with a "take it or leave it" lowball. Granted, these sharks do offer people life-changing business opportunities, but their methods are sometimes pompous and condescending. It's amazing what some people will put up with just to be a part of the Fortune elite. Everyone wants to have stock in the fiscal machine.

America—in spite of its many flaws—is a paradise of opportunity. The American dream remains an attainable reality for anyone willing to invest their sweat equity toward its pursuit. Our government offers us so much aid and assistance in our times of need that even the poorest among us have it far better than some of the more privileged of those in developing countries. The true hustlers and go-getters don't even need a college education to earn six-figure incomes. In America, everywhere you look, there is money to be made. The American dream becomes tainted when we start to take more than we need, and greed takes over. Capitalism has us playing a real-life game of *Monopoly* through investments, scams, and fraud. This toxic capitalist culture we've created is the reason we'll never be satisfied.

It's the running of the bulls and bears as we trample each other to get to the prize. Toxic corporate culture encourages us to sabotage our colleagues for financial advancement. Money, indeed, is the root of all evil. The truth is, greed isn't good. In fact, it's one of the seven deadly sins. It's an ugly, selfish character defect. Those who say that greed is good are only trying to excuse themselves for being miserly corporate psychopaths. At the end of life, God won't care about how much money you made. Forsaking your parsimonious righteousness, what are you giving back in the name of philanthropy and benevolence? You have millions of dollars, but what is your worth? If you're nothing without money, you're nothing with it.

FABIAN M.C. KUYKENDALL

## *Economic Echo: The Cycle of Recession*

The Great Depression of the 1930s set the foundation for The Great Recession of 2008. The Covid pandemic of 2020 gave way to what would become yet another recession. It's a perpetual cycle of cataclysm and economic crisis marked by widespread panic, market crashes, and inflation.

It seems like poetic justice when capitalism leads to an economic downturn. The worst perpetrators have to deal with greed-induced bankruptcy. Unfortunately, the rest of us have to deal with foreclosure, unemployment, and federal assistance like welfare and Medicaid. Many of us live paycheck to paycheck and have no safety net for when disaster strikes. No matter how we try to be prepared for the worst, we seem to end up asking ourselves, "What am I going to do now?"

Our national debt is over $30 trillion, the largest in the world. We're constantly borrowing from—and depending on—other countries like China, Japan, and the U.K. Because of this, the taxpayers have to pay more for less government services. The American government has clearly set a poor example for its citizens. We've adopted a shameless lifestyle of financial irresponsibility. It seems like profligacy and intemperance is the accepted American way. When will we stop being China's bitch and stop using the world as our international credit card?

Our economy is designed to keep us in debt. From credit cards to bank and federal loans, there's always a hole for us to fall into. Credit cards have been one of the most convenient scams since their inception. They entice people to spend more than they need to while paying off the balance monthly—along with a fee—in order to build their credit. Student loans have also been called scams as—due to high interest rates—many borrowers end up having to pay almost twice what they originally owed. For many of us, it can take decades to pay off student loan debt. It's not a good feeling to graduate college owing tens of thousands of dollars before you've even secured a job.

The economic waters are infested with loan sharks who take advantage of desperate individuals seeking payday and title loans. These predatory lenders offer inflated interest rates and deceptive, unfair practices to their ill-informed prey. Our economic system has made it almost impossible for us to avoid incurring debt. You even have to be in debt just to build credit. On top of that, we all have the financial burdens of monthly bill payments including rent, phone, energy, internet, car insurance, the list goes on. Every company wants a piece of your paycheck every month. Even philanthropic causes don't want to settle for a one-time donation anymore; now, every payment has to be recurring.

Of the 730+ billionaires in America, only about ten are Black. Needless to say, there's a very noticeable racial disparity when it comes to wealth. This can be attributed to a number of things, but all roads eventually lead to racism. Black people have to face income inequality, housing/property discrimination, redlining, and urban decay—not to mention neocolonialism in the form of gentrification, which pushes Black people and other minorities out of their neighborhoods. Historically, efforts by Black people to build independent wealth have been sabotaged by White supremacists like those who burned down Black Wall Street, terrorizing the Black residents of the Greenwood District during the Tulsa massacre of 1921.

For decades, Black farmers have been victims of agricultural racism. They've not only been discriminated against by the USDA, they've also been exploited for lower wages than their White counterparts. Black farmers are routinely excluded from government loans and farm subsidies, not to mention emergency assistance and disaster relief. There's an ongoing effort to impede our land retention and economic development. It's infuriatingly disrespectful that America would have the gall to attempt to shut Black people out of the farming industry, especially after hundreds of years of our forced farming labor—we weren't free, so we had to work for free. The more things change, the more they stay the same.

It is widely believed that Dr. Martin Luther King Jr. was assassinated not because he simply had "a dream," but because he spoke about economic equality. At the Grio Awards in 2022, Black real estate entrepreneur and activist Don Peebles shed light on the staggering financial disparity between White men and minorities, calling it "economic apartheid." It's important for Black people to realize the expropriation of Black wealth that continues to rob us of the economic equality of which Dr. King spoke. Ownership is essential to economic inclusion, so we can't continue to sell away our dreams or allow White people to buy us out. We relinquish control and future possibilities when we put money over principle.

Mainly because they are the beneficiaries of inherently racist privilege, many White people have been able to build generational wealth. The passing down of old money to new generations is how the rich stay rich. Many White people depend on our ignorance, it's how they were able to keep us enslaved long after slavery was abolished. For Black people, education is key. It starts with developing financial literacy. By knowing how to properly handle money, we'll be able to build and pass down our own generational wealth—one that can withstand any threat of bigotry.

As a nation, it's time for us to break the cycle. If we've learned anything from past recessions, then history shouldn't have to continue repeating itself.

### *Poison Apple: The "Big Brother" of Big Business*

The value of tech titan Apple Inc. reached $1 trillion in 2018, $2 trillion in 2020, and $3 trillion in 2022. The first to reach these benchmarks, Apple is the world's most valuable company. They've conquered capitalism—an engine of inequality—and used it to promote materialism. Apple is the king of consumerism. They've always seemed to have an arrogant audacity. They appear to have a monopoly on the tech industry, or—at least—that seems to be their agenda.

Their ever-growing product line includes the iPhone, iPad, MacBook, AirPods, and the Apple Watch, which—along with heart rate—seems to monitor everything about its wearer. The future of Apple products looks to be in the form of "wearables." After the watch, the next wearable device will likely be augmented reality (AR) smart glasses. Following this ocular breakthrough, I wouldn't be surprised if Apple invented a need for smart apparel. Eventually, we will all become walking billboards for Apple. Apple will probably be the first company to use microchips to turn humans into actual computers.

Apple not only programs computers, they've programmed us. They've mastered the art of mind control, turning everyday people into hypnotized drones. The brand loyalty of their customers is cult-like. Apple has trained its consumers to buy its products—namely iPhones—multiple times per year. Even the slightest change in design or color is enough to convince the brainwashed masses to rush to the stores for the latest model. These devoted worshipers wait in blocks-long lines for hours just to touch the hem of their master's garment.

On January 22, 1984—during Super Bowl XVIII—Apple aired its instant-classic television commercial, "1984." In the ad—inspired by the George Orwell novel *Nineteen Eighty-Four*—Apple attempts to save humanity from the conformity imposed by "Big Brother" with the launch of their Macintosh PC. They portend, "... you'll see why 1984 won't be like *1984*." My, how times have changed. I don't know if Apple had a hidden agenda from the beginning, but they've turned into the very thing that they warned us against in that illustrious commercial. Apple is now the "Big Brother" of big business; damn, the irony.

Their agenda is becoming clearer. They're pushing their influence beyond tech and into politics in order to profit from power under the guise of business. They had an alleged collaboration with PRISM, a surveillance program headed by the National Security Agency (NSA). Most Apple products are alleged to be made in China for cheap sweatshop labor. They've also faced criticism for unethical business practices and insufficient data security. Somehow, it wouldn't surprise me if their next move was developing a pill that modifies behavior with the promise of giving the user an internal multi-sensory smart device experience.

Apple seems to be pushing dangerously close to an ambition of totalitarianism. They depend on our "unification of thoughts" for their profit. The Apple store isn't as much of a store as it is a place of worship. It's been said that if aliens invaded our planet, they would think that we're under the spell of our devices. I think that's exactly what Apple wants: to keep us staring at our iPhone, iPad, and MacBook screens like mindless minions staring at "Big Brother."

# CHAPTER 12 - SCIENCE & TECHNOLOGY

*Transhumanism: Man's Transformation into a Cyborg Society*

Technology seems determined to eliminate the need for human activity by replacing it with robotics. We have robots that clean our homes for us, robots in the form of cars that drive for us, and robots in the form of machines that result in layoffs for thousands of factory workers. It isn't far-reaching to think that in a couple of centuries, robots will completely replace humans, or maybe—with our robotic obsession—we'll find a way to transform ourselves into cyber beings.

People don't want to be human anymore, we want to be robots. There's an ever-growing community of biohackers who enhance their bodies through the implantation of cybernetic devices. These "grinders" attempt to create immortality by transforming themselves into post-human beings. The transhumanism movement even goes as far as DNA editing. There are CRISPR (clustered regularly interspaced short palindromic repeats) kits available online that are easily accessible to anyone. These kits allow people to experiment with genetic self-engineering like mad scientists in a comic book.

Transhumanism allows us to robotize ourselves, while artificial intelligence (AI) allows us to anthropomorphize objects. AI is the literal personification of technology. It is the embodiment of everything that represents the future. In addition to IoT (Internet of things) robots and voice and face cloning apps, AI has also penetrated the world of adult entertainment in the form of cyberdildonics. This technology allows users to have "virtual intercourse" with an online partner. Of course, there has also been the development of sex robots, which threatens to be a common replacement for human intimacy in the not-so-distant future.

There's a growing belief that AI computers and robots will eventually overtake the human race, so why do we keep evolving the very thing that will eliminate us? Experts and researchers are foretelling a doomsday outcome if we don't "shut it all down" immediately. There are AI tools that are designed to learn software and continue becoming more advanced on their own, which is terrifying. AI and automation are gradually displacing jobs, while AI tools like ChatGPT are helping students cheat by passing off AI-generated content as their own. No one has to work or think anymore.

Because people would rather live in a virtual reality, the Metaverse was created. The Metaverse was supposed to be a world-changing VR dimension; instead, it plays host to a network of racist, misogynistic, sexually depraved losers who now have yet another platform on which to commit their crimes against humanity. There have been many reported instances of assaults in the Metaverse, but—in a virtual world—anything goes. So much for escapism. Personally, I think that we should work on improving reality instead of using technology to run away from it.

Technology moves at a dizzying pace. Every day, we replace our disposable trends. As yesterday ends, it becomes obsolete. Today is tomorrow exchanged with receipt. Because of technology, everything about the future seems cold, soulless, and dystopian. It's ironic how the ultra modern minimalist aesthetic is powered by maximum technology. In this digital age, technology is applied to everything. We can even make food through 3D printing using meat cells. Like most of the latest advances in technology, however, just because we can doesn't mean we should.

The AI Armageddon is upon us as science fiction has turned into reality. We are gradually becoming androids—numb walking barcodes completely devoid of emotion. We're a society of cybernetically-enhanced bodies and autotuned voices devolving into a mirage of what humanity used to be. We've taken the form of holograms like dead entertainers to star in the alternative reality show of deep fake videos. I believe that we have a disturbing future ahead of us, one where we'll constantly have to question what's real.

## *Digital Eye: Cyber Spying & Mass Surveillance*

Privacy has gone extinct. No matter who you are, no matter where you are, the world is always watching you through a digital eye. From *eye*-phones to *eye*-pads, electronics seem obligated to include a camera. This camera is an aperture—an iris that stares through the peephole of the world. For some reason, we have a perverse compulsion to observe other people's private moments. Technology ensures that every moment is watched, which summons paranoia. Some people—including myself—have found it necessary to blindfold every personal digital eye by covering it with tape. With everything that you do, you have to remember: The devices have eyes.

The wave of the future is artificial intelligence. This lucrative concept has scientists and engineers rushing to conceive eerily anthropomorphic talking robots. These seemingly freethinking cyborgs are a drastic leap forward from Siri and Alexa. Technology has even anthropomorphized electronics and appliances. From smart televisions to smart refrigerators, these items have been programmed to talk, think, and watch you at all times. This has quickly become a disturbing trend, one where privacy invasion disguises itself as innovation. When we assign artificial intelligence to inanimate objects, we open the door to a world of perpetual surveillance.

Google seems to have a creepy ambition to be all-knowing and omnipotent. From their nosy information collecting to their intrusive digital advertising, they're determined to be aware of every aspect of your life. They've even programmed us to talk to Google Assistant to ensure that the mic is always on. This makes it easier for them to eavesdrop on intimate conversations that reveal private details about our lives, which they use to manipulate us. "Hey Google, why the fuck are you spying on me?!" Every search you make, every shit you take, they'll be watching you!

There are so many parasitic apps we use—American and international—that collect our data. We download these apps and give them permission to access all of our personal information without giving it a second thought. Many people use home automation to keep an eye on their neighborhood, but fail to realize that it's keeping an eye on them too! The whole obsession with the Internet of things (IoT) is dangerous because it forces you to relinquish privacy, and relinquishing privacy means relinquishing security—which is ironic when you have a smart home security system.

Big data companies use the guise of analytics and algorithms to spy on the masses. They buy and sell our personal data through surveillance capitalism, commodifying our individual information while violating our right to privacy. They're known for working with corporations, politicians, and law enforcement, whom they help engage in biased, unethical policing practices. With every electronic device we use, we leave a digital trace, which will ultimately be used against us.

Spy culture is so prevalent that people actually think it's normal. Aside from businesses tracking our every move on the internet, people put tracking devices on phones, cars, computers, etc. There are invasive, spying drones hovering above our heads and homes like birds of prey. Our everyday electronics scan our identity through face and voice recognition and fingerprinting technology. Employers commonly use their position of authority to spy on their employees through company-issued phones and computers. Why is this so easily accepted? Am I the only one who's terrified about what spy culture can turn into?

It feels like we're only a few years away from a dystopian, totalitarian, Orwellian world of mass surveillance. I'm sure that as we watch *Big Brother*, "Big Brother" is watching us. It seems like only a matter of time until they implant us with microchips and our thoughts are detected by the "Thought Police." Our thoughts truly are the only privacy we have left. No matter where you go in the world, there are hidden cameras and microphones. We all have become cast members of *The Truman Show*, wandering through a hyper-alternative reality, completely oblivious to the voyeurs on the other side.

## *Check Engine: The Climate Change Crisis*

Mother Earth is running a fever. Some people call it global warming, others say that there's nothing to worry about. However, the melting ice caps, rising sea levels, shrinking lakes and rivers, boiling oceans, heat domes, record-high temperatures, turbulent weather, droughts, and wildfires say that there's an ecological crisis happening right now.

It's easy to see how drastically Earth has changed and how dire the current situation is when you look at what it used to be. The rising sea levels are slowly drowning acres of land. Six U.S. states are projected to be partially underwater by 2050. Oceans are becoming acidic, killing growing numbers of fish and other marine life. We're littering our neighborhoods and parks with trash, turning once-beautiful landscapes into landfills. We're also contaminating our waters with trash and oil, and—with carbon dioxide pollution—we're literally poisoning the air.

Climate change affects the earth, our food, and the weather as all things work together. We know that fossil fuel combustion creates greenhouse gas emissions—which is the main cause of global warming—but we still underutilize alternative energy sources. There's no reason the world can't come together and agree upon a universal solution, especially after the success of the Montreal Protocol for ozone depletion. We're rapidly approaching irreversible global tipping points, so why not prevent them while we still can? It doesn't cost a thing to care.

It's amazing how so many politicians can just write off this very real problem. They'd rather pretend that it doesn't exist just because it requires too much of their effort and concerned taxpayers' dollars to fix. It's easier for them to just slap the "fake news" label on it. There's no rational reason for why people make climate change a conspiracy. It's sad that they don't seem to care about the state of Earth that will be left for their descendants. This planet is home to us all, so why wouldn't we want to preserve it?

Global warming is a global warning. Earth is dying all around us as we inhabit it. The time is now for all of us to take responsibility and save this planet. We all can play a part by reducing our carbon footprint, recycling, and through water and energy conservation. Let's join the green movement of environmentalism for the sake of ecological integrity, free of politics. It's not about hugging trees, it's about helping to make a cleaner, more sustainable world.

The check engine light is on. When you ignore this in your personal vehicle, there's only a matter of time before it breaks down. It's easy to ignore climate change because we may think that it doesn't affect us personally, but if Earth is overheated—just like with your vehicle—something is wrong.

# CHAPTER 13 - INSPIRATION & MOTIVATION

*Mental Makeover: Changing Your Thoughts for Positive Results*

Religion—to me—is simply that which we choose to believe. When the same logic is applied to our daily lives, we can control our mindset and create positivity for ourselves. Therefore, if we choose happiness over misery, we'll be happy, and if we believe that we can accomplish our goals, we will. It really is that simple. We have to stop complicating our possibilities and make them possible. We have to look through the optics of optimism because optimism creates opportunity.

When life offers us a sunny day, we should take advantage of it while we can. Time moves faster every day as the days seem to get shorter and shorter. Time moves so fast that we often don't realize it. Sometimes, it feels like we age without getting older, which allows life to sneak up on us, even pass us by. We have to remember that we only have now. The past is gone forever, and the future remains uncertain. We only get one chance at life.

We should always wake with a purpose, even if we don't have plans for the day. We should allow a daily routine to be the motivation that we use as a jump start. The sun is energy to use at our disposal as incentive to rise with it every morning. We should endeavor to gain a victory every day. Success breeds success. We should exploit even the smallest successes in order to build an unstoppable momentum. Everything has an expiration date and we can never be sure of when that date is, so we shouldn't push our luck. We have to act on opportunity the moment that we recognize it.

It's important to recognize what's accessible to you in life and to take advantage of it without taking it for granted. We often put limits on ourselves for which we blame the world. It's a convenient excuse, but the truth is that you're only limited by what you allow in your mind. For instance, when you're in an argument with someone and you *know* that you're right, there isn't a motherfucker alive who can tell you that you're wrong. Whether you are, indeed, right or wrong, it's your conviction that gives you that victory. If you believe in something strong enough, no one can deny you of it.

It's ironic that people seem to think that you're not "living" unless you're doing something detrimental to your life like drinking alcohol, doing drugs, being promiscuous, or any other dangerous activity. Living your life is not about risking your life. It's about sharing your life with others and making their lives better. If you don't do something to enrich the world in this lifetime, then you won't complete your mission as a human being. You can't just show up, eat up all of the food, and then leave; you have to feed some people too.

At some point, we have to stop looking for ourselves and, instead, design ourselves as we wish to be. Sometimes, you have to manipulate people's perception of you. Whether it's the clothes that you wear or the parts of your personality that you choose to highlight, it's how you present yourself that tells people how you want to be seen. If you don't fit in, you might as well stand out. There's only one person who can be you, so it might as well be ... you! The good thing is, you already have the genetic makeup for it.

Sometimes, doesn't it feel like people go out of their way just to get in yours? When it comes to societal behaviors, it's often about intention vs. perception. You should never assume that you know what someone's intentions are because those intentions are usually quite different than what we perceive them to be. We can't control other people, and we can't read their thoughts, so we should do ourselves a favor and stop assuming the worst of each other. We have to learn to see each other for who we really are instead of just casting immediate judgment. At the very least, we can save ourselves so much undue stress.

Sanity is being able to consistently distract and detach yourself from your mind. It's being blissfully unaware of negative thoughts and anxiety. Indeed, ignorance is bliss. You have to be careful what you allow in your mind. Don't create bad energy for yourself. Doomscrolling through the timelines of social media is never good for your mental space. There's always bad news and worse people ready to project their misery onto you. Don't let people control you with their words, never give them that power. There's less traffic on the high road, so don't let pride detour your journey. Happiness is a choice. Misery is a choice. No one can make us upset, we *choose* to be. We can't choose how we feel, but we choose how we react.

Why do we—whether knowingly or unknowingly—base our decisions on what society thinks? You're the only one who has to live *your* life, so why should outside influence be a factor? Aside from social media and everyday culture, we frequently seek guidance by purchasing self-help books, listening to "Ted" talk, or asking Iyanla to *Fix My Life*. Everyone seems to be a life/success coach or motivational speaker who has all of the answers and knows exactly how you should live your life. The problem is, we can never seem to take our own advice. We should worry about fixing our own lives before telling people how to fix theirs.

The most painfully frustrating thing is wanting to change your life for the better—and knowing exactly what you need to do to make that change—but not being able to find the motivation to do it. You shut down mentally and physically and retreat from active productivity just to avoid a potential letdown. Your mind becomes inundated with excuses, which you use to justify your behavior. Therefore, you must avoid excuses at all costs. Excuses are limitations. We have to train ourselves to stop saying "I can't" or anything that negates possibility. Instead of "I can't," it should be "I can." Instead of "if," it should be "when." Instead of "I'll try," it should be "I will." Because words have power, we should always be mindful of what we say and what we think of ourselves and others.

We have to stop talking ourselves out of our blessings. Being our own worst enemy gets us absolutely nowhere. After enough failure, we have to say "fuck fear," "fuck excuses," and allow ourselves to succeed. You learn more from your losses than you do from your wins; therefore, a loss is never a loss unless you fail to absorb the lesson that it provides. Also, we should never let our age determine how far we should be in life. As long as we are living and able, it's never too late to succeed. It's time to stop putting ourselves on society's timetable. Measuring our lives to others will always be an inaccurate comparison because—no matter how it appears—everyone lives a different life.

I believe that God gives us pain with a purpose. You don't make the sacrifices, the sacrifices make you. No one goes around adversity, you have to go through it. When you run away from a problem, you're only running toward another one. You've survived every tribulation you've faced thus far, so you already know how capable you are. Be inspired. Don't just wait for inspiration, seek it if need be. When you're inspired, you become an inspiration for others.

There's so much to be said for the way that we treat each other. We expend so much energy creating ways to degrade and eliminate each other. We shouldn't be a threat to each other's survival. We shouldn't be controlled by hate. In every aspect, hate hurts. It's emotionally, spiritually, even physically exhausting. Let's give ourselves a break, get over our hate, and move on from it. The lesson to be learned from any war is that violence can't create peace. Like water to fire is love to hate. Maybe one day we'll love ourselves enough to love each other.

It's time to make love go viral. Let's start a love pandemic through acts of kindness, paying it forward, and loving those who seem to hate us. Karma is real, and love is a cyclical energy—a centripetal force. Ultimately, a better world is the result of a better you. Of course, it's cliché, but your life really can be whatever you want it to be—as long as you believe that it can be. When you think about it, changing your life could be as simple as changing the way you think.

### *Reality Tells the Truth: The Brutal Honesty of Life*

There isn't any place in the world that's sunny a hundred percent of the time. Sunshine has to be balanced with darkness so that we can appreciate it. The sun is always shining, even when it's not shining on you. The world revolves so that others can shine too.

People say that failure is not an option, but it's a reality. In order to succeed, you have to be willing to fail. You have to distinguish the area between being realistic and relying on hope. It's superstitious to be superstitious. Life happens the way it wants to, no matter how your superstitions try to interfere. Since you have control over you, stop making it necessary for you to start over. You have to find your way out of that vortex of cyclical mistakes because a mistake repeated becomes a lifestyle.

Continue to utilize and appreciate your gifts. Don't be upset with the world if those gifts don't bring you the fame and fortune to which you feel entitled. Success is not reserved for you due to any greatness you may feel that you have. At some point, it's best to realize and accept that you probably won't be as successful as you hoped you would be. This isn't to say "don't dream," but you have to find a way to be okay with your dream not coming true.

It's pointless to question life because it will never make sense. Instead of trying to make sense out of life, it's better to just live it to its fullest. Realize how short life is *before* it starts to decline. Life is a journey, not a destination, so enjoy the moments you're given and don't make fulfillment your goal. Fulfillment is an endless, useless quest. You will never be fulfilled, nor should you strive to be because once you are, there's no reason to live. You should strive to be happy. It's more than possible to be happy without being fulfilled.

Living your life shouldn't be contingent upon who lives it with you. If you need a partner to complete you, then you will never be more than half of a person. You have to be the best version of yourself to be able to deal with those whom you allow in your life. You also have to be careful whom you allow in your life because they may not want to leave. You learn someone's true character when you don't give them what they want. When you distance yourself from people you've outgrown, they say that you've changed. What they don't realize is that you're *supposed* to change. Life demands evolution, you either grow or you die.

In life, there will be people who won't like you simply because they don't want to. The sooner you can understand and accept this, the less time you'll waste being nice to them. Some people aren't secure enough within themselves to embrace and project positivity. So many of us actively surround ourselves with drama and negativity. Living in negativity is like living in filth. Some people fill their homes with trash, mud, sludge, and shit, and others just build their homes on top of landfills. Why would you want to live like that? Negativity relies on our attention to maintain its power; therefore, you should only give attention to that which you want to grow.

People who play dumb aren't playing. It's pointless to engage in a battle of wits with those who are ill-equipped. In most cases, ignorance is willful. People are ignorant not because they simply don't know, but because they *choose* not to care. Don't disappoint yourself by expecting others to live up to your standards. As a rule, people will always let you down—not because they want to, but because no one can be exactly who you want them to be. You don't have to meet anyone's expectations, so why would you expect them to meet yours?

Some men act as if women owe it to them to meet their specific standard of beauty. You don't owe perfection to anyone. We have to stop disguising our insecurities as perfectionism and projecting them onto others. Looks aren't everything, and they don't last forever. At some point, we all become weather-beaten, so why do we criticize each other for it? It's a shame what life does to a person that makes them appear used and less desirable. Physical perfection is beyond human capability. Pretentious is the expectation of perfection from oneself or anyone else. The moral of this story is: Stop chasing perfection, you'll never catch it.

Some women will forgo their own happiness just to deny a man of theirs. Spite and resentment are toxic. More importantly, they only affect you. You can't ingest poison and expect it to kill someone else. You have to know that there's happiness for you in this world. Go claim that happiness and stop trying to take someone else's. Also, don't give your happiness away. Some women prioritize the happiness of a man at the expense of their own. They too often lower themselves to a man who demands their respect. However, a real man doesn't need to demand respect. He is willingly given respect based on his character and his actions—simply by being respectable.

If you use child support money to support yourself, you're a deadbeat parent. The same applies if you refuse child support money out of spite. That money is intended to do exactly as it says: support the child. It's irresponsible and selfish if you deny them that support. You can be wealthy and still be a deadbeat parent. In the end, a child doesn't remember all of the money and gifts that you gave them as much as the attention and time that you invested. Don't make your parenthood their problem either. Your children don't owe you anything for fulfilling your obligation of raising them.

It's your job as a parent to brainwash your child before someone else does. This means instilling the right morals and giving them the tools that they need to get through life. You have to raise and teach them through your actions. You can't create your child's personality, you can only nurture who they already are. Parents: Please stop trying to force your kids to be who *you* want them to be. Just like you, they're the only ones who have to live *their* lives, so they should be able to do so as they choose.

Why do so many of us use the "I'm human" excuse for our mistakes and failures? Of course, you're human; we're all human, and humans make mistakes. Stating the obvious only makes you look less than smart. Nevertheless, many people feel the need to impress others with an image of physical strength or imagined perfection while calling themselves a "beast" or a "machine;" but as soon as they make a mistake, they're conveniently "human" again. Power is for the weak. The truly powerful need not seek it. Humble yourself before life does it for you.

Too many of us lack empathy. We aren't willing to put ourselves in each other's shoes because we don't want someone else's problem to become our problem. I get it: Why concern yourself with things that don't concern you? We make a bad habit of forcing our involvement in the private affairs of other people, some of whom we don't even know. I think that most of us just love digging to find out if other people are as miserable as we are. We have to remember that everyone has problems, no matter how perfect or happy some people may seem. We also have to stop making other people a factor in how we feel about ourselves.

Don't deprive yourself of the advice that you give to other people. Also, if you can't accept your own advice, then keep it to yourself. You're more flawed than you think you are. Stop lying to yourself. If you think that self-help media is a cure-all, stop kidding yourself. You have to be able to detect the bullshit, even if it applies to what you're reading right now. Only ingest what works for you and filter out the rest. More importantly, stop looking for life-changing affirmations by which to live your life.

## *For Every Ebony: An Ode to Black Women*

The most disrespected, unprotected, neglected, and rejected being on this earth

What is her Black life worth?

Unappreciated, underrated, always underestimated

All that you go through, I don't know how you do it

You're my mother, my sister, my auntie, my niece

You're my grandma, my cousin, my daughter, my queen

And I love you, I see you; I know it's hard to be you

But you've grown through all the showers, now it's time to give you your flowers

You're beautiful, intelligent; you're powerful in your element

You're full of grace, you're elegant; the truest woman there's ever been

You're necessary, you're relevant; a masterpiece to revel in

I thank God for you, you're heaven sent; there's magic in your melanin

You've never given up when you had every reason to

No one else is strong enough to go through what you do

You're tough as mahogany and sweet as molasses

They try to take your dignity, but you rise above the impasses

You're a survivor, the world on your shoulders

Enduring it all with the soul of a soldier

In the midst of a hurricane, somehow you remain still

Even if the world doesn't love you, I always will

# FABIAN M.C. KUYKENDALL

For every Ebony burdened by this world

Just know you're more than enough exactly as you are

And you'll forever be heavenly, believe in nothing less

Because you're more than enough

No matter what, just know that you are loved

You are mother Africa, you birthed civilization

It's your birthright to ascend up to the highest elevation

You're a lioness, protect your pride; you're a woman king, so dignified

But you don't have to be modest; there's God in you, you're a goddess

The true standard of beauty, it emanates from the inside

Your design is effortless, you're excellence personified

You're a black diamond, black pearl, and you shine for every Black girl

With bronze skin, you're God-made, and you're beautiful in every shade

From butterscotch yellow to dark chocolate brown

Not a hair out of place on your gold-plaited crown

Your warm glow is love swept like a Serengeti sunset

With Nubian features, true class, everyone wants what you have

Thank you for blessing the world with your presence

What a privilege it is just to bask in your essence

You're stronger than you should have to be, a constant battle uphill

Even if the world doesn't love you, I always will

For every Ebony burdened by this world

Just know you're more than enough exactly as you are

And you'll forever be heavenly, believe in nothing less

Because you're more than enough

No matter what, just know that you are loved

I celebrate you because you deserve it

A woman of quality, a woman of service

You're essential, you're worthy for all that you do

The world wouldn't run or revolve without you

You're beautiful, intelligent; you're powerful in your element

I'm proud of you, you represent the epitome of Black excellence

I appreciate and respect you, I'll defend your honor and protect you

For you, I just want to be everything that you've been to me

You're my home and my purpose; my life, you fulfill

Even if the world doesn't love you, I always will

For every Ebony burdened by this world

Just know you're more than enough exactly as you are

And you are everything I'll ever need, I'll never go astray

Because you're more than enough

No matter what, just know that you are loved